HALL OF FAME
COMPANIES SEARCHING FOR EXCELLENCE IN DESIGN
A REVIEW OF THE 20TH CENTURY

VOLUME 1
EDITED BY PETER ZEC
ON BEHALF OF ICSID

reddot edition

Hall of Fame

Companies Searching for Excellence in Design
A Review of the 20th Century

Review

Preface Peter Butenschøn	8
In Search of Success with Design – **Learning from Best Practice** Peter Zec	10
The Emergence of the Industrial **Design Profession in the United States** John Heskett	16
Defining Design in the 20th Century Conway Lloyd Morgan	22
The Development of Industrial **Design in Asia** Darlie O. Koshy, Singanapalli Balaram	25

Companies

A&E Design	32	Mono	104
AEG	36	Niessing	106
Alcatel	38	Nissan	108
Blanco	40	Nya Nordiska	114
Burkhardt Leitner constructiv	42	O Luce	118
Crown	44	Propagandist	120
DaimlerChrysler	46	Rado	122
Duravit	50	Randstad	128
Electrolux	54	Samsung	134
Fiskars	58	Schwan Stabilo	140
Grupo Di	60	Sedus	142
Herend	64	Siemens	144
IBM	68	Sony	146
iittala	72	Studio Idea	152
Intra	74	Tata	154
Irizar	76	Toyota	156
Jacob Jensen Design	78	Tupperware	162
Kärcher	84	Vivero	166
LG Electronics	86	Vorwerk	170
Ludwig	92	Yamaha	172
Mabeg	96	ZAG Industries	174
Makio Hasuike	98	Zucchetti	178
Miele	100	Zumtobel Staff	180
Molteni	102		

ICSID

International Council of Societies of Industrial Design

ICSID – A Global Network for Design	184

ICSID – Listings

The Executive Boards	186
Professional Members	192
Professional/Promotional Members	194
Promotional Members	195
Educational Members	198
Associate Members	200
Corporate Members	202
Companies – Contact Details	204
Publication Details	207

REVIEW

Preface

by Peter Butenschøn, ICSID President 2001-2003

Architect educated at Cambridge University, Georgia Tech and Harvard University. Associate Professor at Oslo School of Architecture. Rector of Oslo National College of the Arts since January 2003. Founder and Executive Director, Institute for Urban Development in Oslo since 1983. Former Director of Norsk Form, Center for Design, Architecture and the Built Environment, Oslo.

How do we measure excellence in design today? Do we have some kind of yardstick, to be used to give us firm answers in a world of staggering diversity? Can we refer to some objective standard when we seek order in the overflow of goods in our markets, much of it simple trash, unfit for durable use by dignified human beings? Probably not. We, in this case meaning designers, have no yardstick. There is no easy way out, no book of ready answers.

In order to orient ourselves in the designed world that surrounds us, we need to pause sometimes and take stock. It seems that, as never before, there is a need for critical distance, for reflection, for a cool look at what is out there, a questioning mind to meet the barrage of influences on our senses. There is clearly a need not just to look at all the answers, but to ask some questions about what it is all for, and what purposes are served. And there is a need to look at what actually works, what seems to succeed, beyond all pretences and hot ambitions and all the selling language that is wrapped around it.

Discussing design has become an increasingly complex affair, since the agenda seems to be shifting all the time. For some years now, branding and logos have been on everyone's lips. Design has to do with communicating identity, of the produced object as well as of the buyer and user. The kids in my family know only too well that when they pay 100 euro for some Nike shoes, they pay only 10 euro or so for the footwear and the rest for the name, the image, the symbolic belonging to the sphere of Nike users. When I buy a chair or a car or a house, even the kids know that I'm not primarily judging practical performance. They assume that all options work well, and that the difference between them lies in the story that is told, in the aesthetic expression of purpose. Not surprisingly, design quality has become the leading edge for competitive industry in the world of high consumption.

And then, the agenda of design seems to shift. The Johannesburg Summit was recently unable to find sufficient common ground for a forceful attack on the mismanagement of world resources. We are not able or willing to apply the knowledge we have, to producing the goods we need without cutting down the world's forests, or transporting clean water to where people need it, or tapping clean energy for all the machines we have designed to make life for ourselves easier or more enjoyable. Many of the Johannesburg issues were design issues, when looking beyond the formalities and the political fist-fights.

The agenda shifts again, as the one-year mark is passed since the September 11 attacks in the US, and normally level-headed commentators claim that the concerns of the design world have now forever changed, 'where security and safety are paramount concerns; where firefighters, police, soldiers and other people in uniform – not the stock jocks on CNBC or the dot.com kids – are our heroes'. Design addresses essential issues of survival, both at the top end and the bottom end of the world order.

And then once more, the agenda seems to shift as yet another technological innovation hits the market and knocks at our imagination, particularly in the field of communication, where it may seem that the world of physical artefacts is becoming obsolete or at least boringly old-fashioned, replaced by the shining world of the virtual, the unseen and the imagined. These changing agendas tell us that design and the designer is now everywhere, and that the importance of what designers work with has never been greater.

ICSID - The International Council of Societies of Industrial Design – sees itself as the only truly international platform for this discussion, across national and professional boundaries. Within the ICSID framework, designers, academics, promotional experts, businesses and governments can discuss issues that confront design and designers, and issues in human society that can be attacked with design competence as a useful tool. ICSID does not present an ideology of design, and it does not conclude any of the ongoing discussions on the agenda. Rather, it is a facilitator for discussion and insight. Having such arenas for discussion and confrontation, for the exchange of ideas and experience, means standing a better chance of seeing the connection between the branding of identity, the Johannesburg challenges, the fight on terrorism following the World Trade Center crash and the technological advances.

ICSID holds no key to the understanding of complex international issues. Perhaps one of the most useful contributions that ICSID can make to the complex challenges now confronting design worldwide, is to present examples of good work. Rather than trying to push specific solutions or priorities, it is meaningful to show good practice. The objective may sound simple: Whatever you do, in whichever field, you should strive for excellence, for making the most out of the opportunities at hand, for driving the solutions as far as possible towards clarity and perfection.

There may be no better way of doing this than publishing collections of good practice. The names of some companies have become synonymous with design excellence. These companies tend to see design as an essential part of their corporate strategy. How do they do it? It is important to collect these stories as documentation of what actually works. Such stories are important resources for the essential debate on design quality, affecting people with needs and desires.

Collecting success stories may seem like a rather modest contribution to the international design scene. On the other hand, good stories well told have often proven able to fuel imagination and foster creativity. Seen this way, the objective of this book is not modest at all.

In Search of Success with Design – Learning from Best Practice

by Peter Zec

Since 1991, Professor Dr. Peter Zec has been President of the Design Zentrum Nordrhein Westfalen, a German design centre with an international reputation. In 1993 he was appointed Professor of Business Communications at the University of Applied Sciences in Berlin. Professor Dr. Peter Zec is creator and founder of the international red dot design award, and the author and editor of numerous publications: Designing Success (1999), German Design Standards (2000), Good Design (2000), including the "Design Innovations Yearbook" and the "International Yearbook for Communication Design".

Over 20 years have passed since Tom Peters and Bob Waterman, then the leaders of an internal McKinsey research group, compiled a report on excellently managed and successful businesses. The significant results of the research project, which was published in 1982 and entitled "In Search of Excellence – Lessons from America's Best-Run Companies" [1], consist in the description of eight fundamental virtues which all the businesses studied exhibited to a greater or lesser extent. Peters and Waterman predominantly identified the basis of these fundamental virtues which determine success in the 'soft' elements of corporate culture, such as the style of management, specialist knowledge, the qualifications of core staff and the way in which the company regards itself. Although the findings of the research project have lost nothing of their relevance to successful business management, they are still insufficient as a final and comprehensive answer to the question of entrepreneurial success strategies. The search for characteristics which contribute to success has in the meantime been further intensified, and it is likely in future, to occupy us more than ever before. In harmony with and as a continuation of Peters and Waterman's search for success strategies, this article is intended to shed light on the characteristics of successful design-orientated corporate management. Companies like IBM or Crown in the USA, iittala or Fiskars in Finland, Sony or Yamaha in Japan and Duravit or Miele in Germany have not only their success in common, but also their orientation towards design as an essential element in the success strategy they pursue. It is interesting to note that the companies are otherwise different in many respects, such as their size or their corporate form.

This can be seen as an indication that success strategies based on design are not tied to any particular size or form of corporate entity, and that the relevant success criteria differ from case to case. Nevertheless, or perhaps for that very reason, the question arises as to whether any fundamental characteristics can be discerned as a common basis for success with design, or, to put it in another way, is it possible to learn from the successful by identifying firm tenets of design management? In the course of over ten years of observation and analysis of companies whose success is essentially based on the continuous pursuit of innovative design concepts,

'IBM T5', personal computer by IBM Corporation, IBM 2001

I have been able to recognise, with significant continuity, seven attributes which successful design-orientated businesses possess and which distinguish them from their less successful competitors. Of course, it also became apparent in the course of those observations that design cannot be deployed as a universal miracle drug to achieve the desired entrepreneurial success. Even if it does not always appear so, success with design cannot be simply achieved off the cuff and with minimal effort, but rather, is based on highly systematic and stringently planned management.

Just as an excellent wine depends on a number of basic factors such as the soil, the position of the vineyard and so on, success with design can only come about under specific conditions. A company which cannot provide those conditions in full will never be able to achieve an outstanding, excellent success with design. In contrast to the vintner, however, who can hardly change anything in the given circumstances of soil, climate or location, businesses are in principle in a position to change themselves thoroughly. The relevant conditions for top achievements in design can then also be created in that way. Accordingly, it is possible for all companies to be successful with design, provided that they want to do so and are prepared to create the appropriate conditions. Those, however, who do not have these good or very good conditions in advance and are not willing to create them by processes of change and renewal have only relatively small prospects of success with design.

Being successful with design does not mean concentrating on a single product or a single segment of the range. The individual product, as good and successful as it may be, does not count initially when the success of the business has to be secured. It happens repeatedly that companies are highly successful with individual products and still cannot survive in the long term. This does not have to affect the entire enterprise as sometimes only individual divisions have to be closed down. One example, is the closure of home electronics production at Braun. The Braun company set new design standards worldwide in the 1960s and 1970s, above all, in the home electronics field. But, in the final analysis, that was still not enough to secure the company's long-term success in that segment. The division was finally closed, even though the design of the products manufactured was convincing right up to the end. The conditions for the success of the company as a whole were simply not fulfilled at that time, and had not been for some while. Good design alone is not sufficient in the long term to ensure survival in a competitive environment.

Design must therefore be seen and practised in the context of corporate management in the broadest sense. It must be remembered that a sick business cannot recover simply through design. On the contrary, the situation with design is more akin to the Latin dictum "mens sana in corpore sano". Successfully managed businesses can either become even more successful with design, or at least preserve the success they have achieved. The best starting point is a synthesis of innovation-orientated and design-orientated management. The foundation stones of corporate success resulting from innovation have already been sufficiently examined by Peters and Waterman. Seven further characteristics can be listed for the success with design that follows, each of them corresponding to the general success criteria. Put in a nutshell, the special achievements of all successful design-orientated businesses become apparent in the following seven criteria.

1. Primacy of quality: "Quality is not a thing. It is an event."[2] With that statement, Robert Pirsig identifies the nature of quality which goes beyond the mere consideration of objects. This is precisely the understanding of quality which prevails in successful design-orientated businesses. Quality, and the special value associated with it, are not given factors in the design of a product, but only result from the mutual relationship between subject and object, between people and products. Only when a specific event or encounter reveals itself as a special experience of use or desire, can one become conscious of the quality and the value which goes with it. A serious striving for quality is a striving for just that experience. At the same time, the fixation on costs is suspended, which does not however, mean that costs per se no longer matter.

'Philippe Starck Edition 2', wash basin designed by Philippe Starck, Duravit 1999
'ESR 4000' lift, lift truck by Crown Equipment Corporation, Crown 2002

In the economy, everything has its price. Objects and services which cost nothing are not part of the economy. Even if we sometimes have the impression of getting something for nothing, we have really already paid for it. In the economy, we are used to dealing with costs and prices without necessarily focusing on quality or indeed considering it at all. Thinking in cost and price categories does not necessarily include quality. The reverse is however not true: thinking in quality terms does not necessarily exclude considerations of costs. They are merely regarded as being of subordinate importance. The ideal is for the highest quality to be offered at the best possible price. This is what outstanding design is concerned with.

Long-term success with design can only be achieved when, on the one hand, the striving for quality always takes precedence over the fixation on costs and, on the other hand, the quality and price of a product are reasonably related. In this way, the experience of quality is, in the final analysis, also influenced by the price. When the price of a product is felt to be too high, that subjectively devalues its quality. Then, what Luhmann so concisely describes actually occurs: "Prices stop people buying"[3] Success cannot be achieved in this way. Successful companies attach great importance to preventing the price from reducing the quality of their products.

2. Motivation – The will to design: The search for the most suitable form is the main driving force behind all innovative and creative actions in the business. The will to design becomes an integral part of the object of the enterprise. The aim is not merely to satisfy a defined demand, but to do so always in the best possible form. There are no projects and no departments within the enterprise that escape this attitude. Just because it is in principle impossible to take optimum decisions in design, it is important for the motivation to design not to subside. Optimum decisions in design matters are impossible because no precise calculations can be performed on simplified models. For that reason, the best that can be achieved is a satisfactory decision. A decision is satisfactory when it closely approximates to the solution of a problem of form in an actual real-life situation. Viewed in this way, „design is a profession and not an exact science."[4]

But, the survival of the profession depends upon commitment and the motivation to renew and reshape existing things again and again, whilst science is based on laws and precise empirical findings.

As no-one can decide with absolute certainty what is right or wrong in design, everything that exists has to be called into question again and again. The process is one of permanent adaptation to real life, and that is in itself, the driving force behind permanent striving for renewal in design. But this motivation is by no means present in all companies. Only the best in their particular industry are driven forward in this way, and that leads to clearly perceptible differences between competitors. While some advance unstoppably in their will to design and their striving for innovation, most of the others wait to see what direction design trends and standards will take, so as to then jump on the bandwagon. But if conditions change more rapidly than they predict, those who hesitate, are in the end left behind.

3. Development of value consciousness: "It is not a question of doing something. It is a question of what you do not do. Then you know what has to be done."[5] Vilim Vasata knows what matters when you want to stand apart from the crowd. One can only recognise individual quality when one sees the mass. "There is no quality without comparative examination."[6] Quality is not a given absolute, but requires constant redetermination. There is a risk here of losing the broad view and betraying principles formerly adopted. The greatest challenge is to follow a line of continuity which others can also see. As, however, no formula for success can be established with mathematical precision, other factors have to come into play when decisions are being taken.

What has to be done, is to make the question of form in design decidable. As it is in principle an irresolvable matter, mathematics, or indeed formal logic, are – as indicated above – of no use. Decisions on design are taken not on paper, but in "visual thinking"[6], where conscious distinctions are made. This demands intensive comparative observation from the decision maker. Successful design-orientated businesses always have an eye on general

design events above and beyond their own activities and their own industry. If they are not to wander off course, their observations have to be conducted in accordance with specified criteria within a framework in which the answers are already defined. The framework is established by a specific value consciousness which is developed within the company on the basis of experience. The observation framework can be generously dimensioned or indeed restricted, depending on the nature of the value consciousness involved. But that is not what matters in the end. On the contrary, the important thing is for a framework in the form of a consciousness of value to be established in the first place. For only in that way is it possible to recognise and decide what one does not want to do, in order, finally, to know what is to be done with design.

By establishing and developing an independent value consciousness, successful companies can come to grips with the problem of determining form. For value consciousness goes hand in hand with a particular method of conferring meaning. As soon as we recognise something as meaningful, we can also discern within it, a corresponding quality. The recognisable meaning gives an action, or the result of making which is manifested in a product, a certain importance which distinguishes it from others.

Companies which are successful with design stand apart from their competitors by being able to give their actions and their products a meaning which is accessible to others and which stems from the special value consciousness of the enterprise. In this way, the companies grow – quite literally – beyond themselves and enable their ideas of value to reach outsiders who either have the same or similar ideas or who immediately recognise a meaning in the manufacturer's activities and products.

4. Communicative action: Problems of corporate management in general, and of design in particular, can be described as problems of communication. In each case it is the form of communication which has a decisive influence on success. This statement implies that communication also has a design dimension which performs a determining function. Well conducted negotiations lead to good results. Successful companies pay great attention to communication, consciously or not, when decisions have to be taken and made comprehensible to staff and stake holders such as customers and suppliers. As a rule, this is only the case when all those involved can discern a common purpose in the relevant actions.

In this context, communication can no longer be seen as the transmission of information from a sender to a receiver. That form of communication must necessarily lead to situations characterised by authoritarian and 'know-all' behaviour on the part of individual participants. In this context, decisions acceptable to all the parties are difficult, if not impossible, to achieve. Usually, one party feels inferior to the other, and so a common direction only emerges as the result of dominant behaviour or even the exercise of power. A joint decision promulgated under these conditions will not normally last for long, as it is really the decision taken by the person who dominated in that particular situation. However, as soon as the situation changes in favour of the underdog, that person will turn their back on the joint decision just as quickly as the person agreed to it under pressure. Most companies are still prone to this form of communication, but it is unsuitable for long-term success with design, as decisions on design have a much greater probability of success when they are based on collaborative working and team work rather than on power.

Companies which are successful with design in the long term practise a form of communicative action which is based on a fundamental freedom of selection by the persons involved. Consciously or unconsciously, communication is then practised in the way Francisco Varela described as ideal, in that, "Communication is rather to be understood as the reciprocal designing and shaping of a common world by common action: we produce our world in common acts of speaking."[7] Communication here does not function as a tool, as a means to an end, but is rather the network or the structure by which each individual and the enterprise as a whole defines itself. This also applies, of course, to the value consciousness manifested in each individual and in the company and the associated demands placed on design.

'Prof Pan', cookware designed by Björn Dahlström, iittala 2002
'AIBO', entertainment robot by Sony Design Center, Sony Corporation 1999

5. Room for creativity: "Freedom is always the freedom of those who think differently." Rosa Luxemburg once represented this radical view of freedom when looking forward to an as yet non-existent form of society. But this form of freedom is still today more the exception than the rule, and this is true for companies as well. People who think differently are not very welcome, because they call the existing state of affairs into question, and by doing so, engender restlessness and insecurity. Those, however, who really do strive for something new, must also be in a position to cast doubt upon existing circumstances and forget what they had once learned was correct. Only under these conditions can creativity develop and flourish.

Creativity itself is not particularly promising in terms of success. There are hosts of people who can be described as highly creative, but are not successful. The decisive factor for the success which can be achieved with creativity is how it is handled. If one gives it unlimited freedom to develop, the result is frequently a growing chaos which gets completely out of control. If, however, creativity can be used to view circumstances and objects from new and changing perspectives with the aim of making new decisions, then it is an indispensable part of success.

The great enemy of creativity is the dogma of tradition. Excessively strict and stringent rules and regulations also place a bridle on creativity. Companies frequently design their products in accordance with strict guidelines in order to avoid potential risks. In the long term, however, this cannot guarantee success. Even in a company like Coca-Cola, eternal success cannot be regarded as a result of holding fast to existing formulae. Although, or perhaps just because the successful product itself cannot really be changed, the Coca-Cola managers are continually engaged in a creative search for alternatives to the existing drink. The involvement of creativity becomes even clearer in the product peripherals and the company's communications.

Every business success, however great and enduring, contains the germ of its own destruction. The more static the behaviour of a company, the greater is the risk that the success will in the future suddenly disappear.

Unintentionally, this behaviour gives competitors the opportunity to copy or imitate decisive characteristics of the success. At first, only small market shares may be sacrificed, but in the end, a downward spiral can set in and lead to unexpectedly large losses.

Companies which are successful with design in the long term provide sufficient freedom for creativity both in their general management and in the field of product development to guarantee permanent change. In doing so, they follow the idea that while it may be possible for competitors to imitate their products, they cannot imitate the power of constant renewal which this freedom for creativity engenders.

6. Daring to experiment: "Nothing ventured, nothing gained." This old proverb applies to companies which always take the safe option and rely on tried and tested concepts. They often pursue a 'me too' strategy, in which they imitate the success of competitors in a safer form. Major successes or leading positions within the industry cannot, however, be achieved without a certain courage to experiment. Where would the automobile industry be today if there had not repeatedly been groundbreaking corporate successes based on daring experiments? More than ever before, such experiments are needed in those industries whose markets are extensively stagnant and saturated.

It is not always necessary to perfect products to a maximum of efficiency. It is more important to design products which can still surprise and astonish us. Products of that kind are not necessarily notable for their highly developed technical perfection, but for their experimental character which appeals to our emotions and awakes a certain desire in us. The jurors of the red dot design award, for instance, could not conceal their astonishment when they were confronted for the first time with the robot-like dog "Aibo" from Sony in the category of home electronics. At the same time, a lively discussion started on the sense and purpose of such a product. At first, some of the jurors were totally disinclined to attribute any value to the product, but gradually, they all came to see it as a daring experiment and a significant innovation for the industry.

[1] Tom Peters, Bob Waterman: In search of Excellence – Lessons from America's Best-Run Companies. Boston: Harper & Row, 1982. / [2] Robert M. Pirsig: Zen and the Art of Motorcycle Maintenance – An Inquiry into Values. New York: Random House Inc., 1976. / [3] Niklas Luhmann: Die Wirtschaft der Gesellschaft. Frankfurt/Main: Suhrkamp, 1994. / [4] Herbert Simon: Sciences of the Artificial. Cambridge: Massachussetts Institute of Technology, 1969. / [5] Vilim Vasata: Radical Brand – Marke Radikal. Munich: Econ, 2000. / [6] Rudolf Arnheim: Anschauliches Denken – Zur Einheit von Bild und Begriff. Cologne: DuMont, 1977. / [7] Francisco J. Varela: Kognitionswissenschafts – Kognitionstechnik. Frankfurt/Main: Suhrkamp, 1990. / [8] Tom Wolfe: From Bauhaus to our House. New York: Farrar, Straus and Giroux, 1981.

Finally, "Aibo" was unanimously selected for the red dot award: intelligent design. Companies which pursue successful design initiatives intentionally back unusual solutions. They have the courage to conduct experiments in order to learn from them and stand apart from the crowd of competitors. Especially in design, experiments of this kind are indispensable to success.

7. Understanding the customer: "The customer is always right." This saying also applies to success with design. But not all companies, by far, are convinced of it. The prevailing attitude in many businesses in Germany in particular, is that customers have to be driven to their own salvation by demanding design concepts. This idea goes back to the teachings of the Bauhaus and the Deutscher Werkbund at the beginning of the 20th century. In his book, 'From Bauhaus to our House'[8], Tom Wolfe harshly criticises the bliss-dispensing pose of the Bauhaus designers. They designed new architecture and new furniture for the workers, without ever considering to ask them what they wanted. The result was merciless rejection of the designs by the very people for whom they were intended. As the Bauhaus example illustrates, it makes no sense to design something which goes over the heads of the users. Companies which are successful with design have learned that they have to create a new world together with their customers, in which not only the manufacturers and designers feel good, but where the customers can also be at home.

Products are, as a rule, intended for use. That use, however, is not always determined by the design, but often by people's habits. One good example of this is the typewriter keyboard. From an ergonomic point of view, it is unusable, as the hands have to adopt a totally unnatural and cramped posture to operate it. Functional reasons however prevented any account being taken of this deficiency in the design of mechanical typewriters for decades. A habit therefore developed and survives to the present day, although it is now perfectly possible to manufacture ergonomically optimised keyboards. Customers simply do not accept them, as the habit acquired over many years is stronger. Numerous attempts by companies to overcome this habit have failed.

Even if customers are not always able to say what they want, they mostly know what they do not want. Anyone who overlooks this runs the risk of missing the mark and building up stocks of unsaleable products. Successful companies, therefore, try to develop their products on the basis of what the customers will accept. They know that there is no point in using design as a means of self-realisation. For in the final analysis, products have to sell. Good design needs success, but in the end, it is the customer who decides what is successful and what is not.

Conclusion: To summarise, success with design can be planned. Nevertheless, that is only possible when the conditions outlined above are met. The companies which are successful with design prove that success has to be carefully prepared. It is by no means sufficient to concentrate on the design of one or more individual products. Just as one swallow does not make a summer, a single, well designed product does not guarantee enduring success in business. That can only be achieved when the company as a whole is in a very good market position. Good design of individual products merely sets off a flash fire which goes out just as quickly as it was ignited. The important thing, on the contrary, is to develop a general consciousness of design within the business, characterised by the seven principles ranging from the primacy of quality and the will to design, through the development of value consciousness and communicative action, to room for creativity, the courage to experiment and understanding of the customer. The size or form of a company does not really matter. It is only important for both the design management and the general corporate management to be on a sound footing. Design management, however seriously applied, cannot compensate for fundamental, commercial deficiencies or omissions. But, well managed businesses can become even more successful with well thought-out design management. This is what we can learn from the companies which enjoy success with design.

The Emergence of the Industrial Design Profession in the United States

by John Heskett

John Heskett is a Professor at the Institute of Design at Illinois Institute of Technology (Chicago, USA). Professor Heskett has earned an international reputation as a scholar of design history, and is the author of, among others, Industrial Design (1980) and Toothpicks & Logos (2002). In addition to writing and lecturing internationally on design, Professor Heskett has acted as consultant to government bodies, educational organisations, and private companies in many countries.

This article first appeared in 'The Alliance of Art and Industry: Toledo Designs for modern America', exhibition catalogue, Toledo Museum of Art, March 24 - June 16, 2002, distributed by Hudson Hill Press, New York.

The Emergence of Industrial Design: In the late nineteenth century, industrialisation transformed every aspect of American life. Changes in technology - machinery, sources of power and raw materials - were important, but it went much further. There were vast changes in communications, in how goods and people were transported and information transmitted, altering perceptions of space and time. Other changes were in economic organisation, business structure and management, in finance and the structure of markets. A swelling flow of goods and services involved complex interrelationships with sweeping patterns of change in society - in the locations in which people aspired to live, the concepts of how they lived, by what values, of how homes were organised and the kind of life considered appropriate for them.

The First World War brought huge wealth to the United States and its emergence as a major world power. The end of the war in late 1918 released a pent-up demand for goods of all kinds. By 1920, a confluence of this remarkable series of changes was occurring. Large business organisations now dominated the American economy and the technology of mass-production and scientific management, based on time and motion studies, was transforming the organisation of work. Electrical power was becoming widely accessible, proving extraordinaryly flexible for both business and domestic uses, and the automobile enlarged individual mobility. A remarkable outcome was a 300% increase in the total volume of manufactures in the U.S. between 1899 and 1929.[1] The proliferation of new products was especially strong in the new field of electrical domestic appliances that began to appear in very substantial quantities by the late 1920s. In 1920, however, the boom ended and the American economy ran into a serious downturn. Many companies had invested huge sums in mass production capacity, requiring heavy interest and overhead costs, while over-optimistic production schedules created large inventories with no way of moving them. Many firms went bankrupt or were taken over. It was a sobering blow to confidence and it is here that the general pattern of development intersected with the specific impact of this economic depression. Above all, the depression underlined that, as a production system, mass manufacture was highly

'Model T' convertible by Ford Motor Company, Detroit 1914

inflexible. It worked most efficiently and economically when large volumes were produced in constant flows. To fundamentally change products required retooling and physically rebuilding production lines, a disruptive, time-consuming and costly process. Demand therefore needed to be effectively managed to keep large quantities of basically identical products selling cheaply. This crisis of 1920-1921 was therefore a turning point in the evolution of American corporations. To avoid being caught again in such a trap, many began developing techniques to accurately forecast future demand and adjust production flows accordingly. The clear logic was that mass production required mass consumption, and public taste had to be shaped accordingly. The concept of a "consumer society" began to emerge.

Advertising, which had earlier emerged in the context of the growth in mass production and a national market, obviously had an important part to play in this scheme. By the early 1920s, advertising practitioners were probing new ways to induce the public to buy. The success of war-time propaganda campaigns in manipulating opinion, backed by psychological theories of subconscious, hidden desires revealed in the symbolic language of dreams, underscored the power of visual imagery as a manipulative tool, which implied a new emphasis on visual form in industrial manufacture. From the recognition of this fact, it was but a short step to refining manufactured forms to present a distinctive advertising image - as modern, attractive, glamourous, convenient, hygienic, new or improved – to enhance marketing potential. This was an important early stage in the emergence of industrial design.

The Growth of In-house Design: If, in general terms, the emergence of industrial design can be seen as part of attempts by mass production industries to assert control over new market conditions, the role of industrial management in this evolution requires recognition. It is often overlooked, however, in favour of accounts emphasising the role of independent consultant designers as some kind of free artistic spirit. Consultants were indeed important figures in this story, but dramatic changes also took place in industrial companies. Indeed, it can be argued that the need for new kinds of design competencies were first articulated in responses of business managers to new competitive conditions. A particularly important example was the role of Alfred P. Sloan in redefining the market for mass-produced automobiles, which powerfully influenced how design developed in corporate contexts.

The initial breakthrough in mass-producing automobiles was, of course, the great achievement of Henry Ford. His immense success lay in producing one basic vehicle, the 'Model T', which, as far as he was concerned, needed no improvement. All that was required was to continually reduce cost. Whether Ford actually uttered the apocryphal statement attributed to him, "You can have any colour you like, as long as it's black," his product philosophy gave it credibility. Ford's approach worked remarkably well for as long as he was the sole mass-producer of automobiles and dominated the market – in other words, while he had no effective competition. When other companies built mass-production facilities, however, the situation became more volatile. That same year, interestingly, also saw the final collapse of 'Model T' sales, primarily under the impact of GM's new strategy. Henry Ford had stubbornly resisted suggestions that appearance mattered in car sales, but now in a humiliating retreat, he was forced to totally close his plants and hastily design and retool for a new car. Ford survived but leadership of the American automobile industry now decisively passed to GM.

As the largest company in the world with an enormous output in its own right, the design methods GM developed dominated not just the U.S. automobile industry, but also many other sectors, most notably consumer appliances. As a concept of design originating in industry, and validated by the most powerful and successful corporation of its time, the influence of styling was powerful and profound. Sloan's widely read autobiography, published in 1963, with a chapter on 'Styling', heavily conditioned the thinking of innumerable executives on what constituted design and how it could be applied in a corporate context. Ironically, however, this was precisely the point at which styling was facing a heavy challenge from new approaches to design developed by overseas competitors.

John Heskett

'Lucky Strike' cigarette packet designed by Raymond Loewy, USA 1947

The Growth of Consultant Design: A second strand of development in the 1920s was in the rapid growth of design consultancies, founded by independent designers whose livelihood depended on providing design services to businesses, and later, in the Second World War, to government clients. They originally shared many methods, concepts and approaches with corporate designers, but a divergence began to occur as consultants gained experience and prestige. They began to see their role in wider terms than that encapsulated in the concept of styling. They came from many backgrounds, but a necessary qualification for success was an ability to work in a commercial context. Of the first generation of designers who emerged in the late 1920s, Joseph Sinel, Lurelle Guild, John Vassos, George Sakier, Walter Dorwin Teague and Raymond Loewy had all worked as commercial illustrators in one form or another. This background also largely explains why designers followed the organisational model of advertising by establishing independent consultancies. Egmont Arens had been a magazine editor, while Norman Bel Geddes and Henry Dreyfuss were well known as theatre designers.

Another source of designers, those from a decorative arts background, specializing in craft-based designs for traditional product areas such as furniture, ceramics and glass, had more mixed fortunes. They tended to remain specialists, adapting their specific skills to particular manufacturing sectors, as with Gilbert Rohde in furniture and Russel Wright in housewares. Some, however, did respond to the breadth of new opportunities, most notably, Donald Deskey.

The influence of commercial applications of design was rapidly growing, however, and was highlighted in Fortune magazine in early 1934. The author, although not credited, was George Nelson, himself to become a leading industrial designer. It drew a distinction between traditional industries - the 'Art Industries', such as textiles, pottery and furniture that had long depended upon appearance for sales - and industrial design. The latter "came into being as mass production raised output to where, one after another, industries hitherto without benefit of other than engineering design found their products matched by other manufacturers, and the market consequently glutted. Furniture and textiles, long taken for granted, had long sold on design. Now it was the turn of washing machines, furnaces, switchboards, and locomotives. Who was to design them?" Nelson's reply to this rhetorical question was: "The product had to be made to sell itself. The designers were called in." The article pinpointed, however, an important feature of how design was evolving, for the men who "came to redesign the surface of the product, often stayed to suggest practical improvements ... ".

A feature of the Fortune article was a list of ten designers, "chosen arbitrarily as typical and illustrative", showing their age, experience, compensation, staff, typical achievements and clients or employers. Norman Bel Geddes had the largest staff, of thirty, while George Sakier was next with eleven. Interestingly, people later considered leading pioneers still had small offices: Henry Dreyfuss had five staff, Teague four, while Raymond Loewy had only one. Project fees ranged for Bel Geddes from $1,000 to $100,000, but an overall mean figure was more in the range of $10-20,000, with consultation rates ranging from $50 per hour (Dreyfuss) to $100-200 per day (Lurelle Guild).

Fortune gave a detailed account of the new profession, citing successful projects resulting in sales and profits being increased and factory costs lowered. Concluding that "industrial design is certainly here to stay in a number of industries that knew it not before", a note of caution was also sounded. Because of the range of individual talents and approaches "the varying methods by which similar products are being designed raises the question of how this designing is going to be done". [2] This arose from the fact that there had hitherto been no common basis of training for designers.

Meeting the growing demand for trained practitioners required an expansion of design education. The bulletin of what was then the Carnegie Institute of Technology in Pittsburgh for 1933-4 had an optional course in Industrial Design taught by Alexander Kostellow that covered "Special problems in the design of textiles and utensils, rendered drawings, details and execution". [3] This was followed by a degree course in Industrial Design, believed to be the first such in the world, established by Robert Lepper in

'Coca-Cola' bottle designed by Alexander Samuelson, 1916

1934. A Carnegie teacher, Donald Dohner, left for New York in 1936 to set up a highly successful industrial design course at the Pratt Institute, where Kostellow later joined him. Many other schools followed their example.

By 1936, Business Week reflected a more sober recognition of the role of design. A two-part article headed: "Not a luxury but an economy, not a fine art but a practical business", [4] used the examples of Dreyfuss' designs for New York Central's The Mercury train and Loewy's streamlined boat for the Virginia Ferry Company to proclaim that "America has definitely become design conscious". Hundreds of manufacturers in many different fields, it asserted, were "being forced to consider product alterations - forced literally into the increased sales and decreased production costs which good design guarantees". [4] However, with design now regarded as a valid business activity, practitioners found it necessary to disabuse manufacturers "of the prevailing idea that design is something of a cross between black magic and refined extortion ... ". [4]

Business Week went into considerable detail to debunk the miracle worker reputation, and justified designers' fees by the range of their work - examining production methods, materials and function, supplemented by marketing research and studies of products in use. Such approaches were moving industrial design far beyond the corporate concept of styling. Well-rounded design service, it said, "embraces virtually every department of a business, even including legal aspects and labour problems". Moreover, design was "proving its power to sell not only articles of merchandise but such intangibles as service and company reputations". The article concluded: "But the soundest foundation on which design builds for the future is its unquestioned ability to determine what the public wants, to build products to meet those demands, to cut cost in the process." [4]

Harold van Doren gave a more skeptical view of how designers were regarded when writing in 1940: "Art, even combined with mechanical ingenuity and merchandising spark, is still suspect with some hard-boiled businessmen. It smacks of afternoon tea and Greenwich Village. Unfortunately there has been just enough slapdash superficiality masquerading as industrial design to give credence to their patently unjust conclusion that the entire brotherhood is a pack of incompetents."

It may be a matter of years before the designer will find his proper level in the kingdom of commerce. To picture him as the saviour of industry, the fair-haired boy with the magic wand who can always make sales curves hit the ceiling, is just as false as the opposite extremes. Somewhere between the two he will find his eventual place. [5]

This last point was probably demonstrated to great effect during the Second World War, when many designers made significant contributions to war projects. In the period after 1945, however, some were to map out a more ambitious scenario for the application of their talents.

Industrial Design and Business Strategy: On April 29th, 1952, at Harvard University's Graduate School of Business Administration, a seminar jointly organised with The Society of Industrial Designers took place on the theme "Linking Business and the Consumer: Case Discussions in Industrial Design". Two sessions featured Procter and Gamble, with Donald Deskey, now Senior Partner of Donald Deskey Associates, and a senior executive from P&G, and Studebaker, with Raymond Loewy similarly partnering corporate executives. [6]

In the 1950s, such events were not unusual. Designers spoke on other occasions at Harvard and other major business schools. In business organisations and publications, they regularly argued their role with clarity and conviction. They had established concepts, methods and a professional style that was appropriate and acceptable in business circles. Neither did their efforts rest there, for ideas about the role of design continued to evolve. In that respect, both Deskey and Loewy provide indicative examples of this new trend in design.

As a furniture designer, Deskey was regarded as one of the best of his generation. By 1937, he was functioning as a design consultant, later with offices on Madison Avenue in New York and top drawer clients.

Lounge chair and ottoman designed by Charles and Ray Eames, 1956

Particularly in the realm of packaging for consumer products his firm shaped many of the most vivid images of the consumer economy. But what is most striking is his thinking about the nature of design as a business and where its future lay. The artist/designer, who in the early 1930s emphasised the need for a national style, now ran a successful consultancy in a highly professional manner. Deskey had clearly developed into a businessman, aware that design processes must involve many disciplines to resolve the problems of satisfying both client and ultimate customer. He provided not only design skills, but was involved in discussions with major clients on future directions affecting their businesses. In addition, he was becoming a spokesman for industrial design at major institutions and events and writing numerous articles articulating ideas about the contribution of industrial design to business and future directions. Deskey's advocacy of design as a high-level activity vital to the competitive future of corporations, and his growing apprehension at the lack of competitiveness in many American firms was shared by Raymond Loewy, who similarly advocated "total planning" as a vital necessity in successfully executing design programmes.[7] He also criticised a tendency of managers to prefer designs that echoed competitors' products, wryly commenting that "timidity and, even less, following-the-leader are not indicative of transcendental executive ability". Loewy also pointed to a decline in American manufacturing quality that disillusioned purchasers, who after being attracted by the external form, found products unsatisfactory in use.

The emphasis on planning was also strongly featured in a review of design in Business Week in 1958: "The 'airbrush boys' of 20 years ago are now up to their ears in long-term planning for their clients." Industrial designers' work was described as extending to shaping whole corporations, reaching through concept, manufacture, distribution and point of sale to the customer. "Many manufacturers", the article continued, "find this breadth the designer's chief asset." The problems of change, however, could not only be attributed to managers. The article noted a degree of confusion in the ranks of designers, particularly those trained and practising in styling-oriented skills, who were uncomfortable with this potentially enlarged role.[8] Such confusion has not been resolved to this day.

Conclusion: In a New Year's review article for Printers Ink in January, 1960, Donald Deskey sounded a prescient warning on another sign of the times. "I believe that 1960 will see an accelerated list of new products on the American scene - but no longer as a near monopoly of American manufacturers. There will be an unprecedented demand on the talents of American industrial designers by foreign manufacturers determined to master techniques that will permit a deeper penetration of the U.S. market." He cited a proposed contract for his firm with a major Japanese corporation. "Requirements are not only for factors of design, product planning, diversification, and packaging, but they go deeper to include information on advertising and merchandising, market potential, mass-production techniques, and even automation." The firm was also prepared to make major investment in production and distribution facilities. It was a proposal, in fact, that neatly illustrated Deskey's concept of long range design planning. The answer, he believed, was for American companies to use creative talent, innovative products and knowledge of their home market to compete effectively. At the same time, he again sounded a warning against the problems of inertia and opposition to change that stood in the way.[9]

Such warnings went largely unheeded, however, and during the 1960s the role played by design in American corporate thinking waned, being widely reduced to executing ideas developed by others. Criticisms of American companies' unwillingness to compete on the basis of a broader understanding of creative ideas at a strategic level subsequently seemed justified as penetration by overseas competitors of the domestic market across a broad spectrum of product categories followed, frequently based on superior design. The consequences of this failure to innovate for communities such as Toledo have been a bitter price to pay. To explain how and why this occurred is not simple. In part, it reflects a sense of complacency arising from the unprecedented success of American industry in the Second World War and the boom years of the 1950s that followed. Another possible explanation is the manner in which quantitative methodology, stimulated by the surge of statistical approaches developed to control the huge logistical problems of the Second World War, came to domi-

'i-Mac G4', computer by Apple Industrial Design Team, Apple Computer Inc., 2002

nate management thinking and business school curricula. New financial techniques and marketing concepts were the beneficiaries and they stressed control rather than innovation. Design, and creative thinking generally, is not easily quantified, however, which sets it at a disadvantage in corporate structures. In his book, The Reckoning, David Halberstam commented on events at the Ford Company in the 1960s and '70s, where "... in most conflicts between the product people and their counterparts in finance, the advantage lay with the finance men. For the product men were arguing taste and instinct, and the finance people were arguing certitudes. It was an unfair match." [10] The prevalence of the concept of styling also played a part in the loss of competitiveness by many American companies. As long as General Motors dominated the home market, and defined the way vehicles were designed for it, styling seemed a recipe for success – particularly since other manufacturers played the game according to the same rules. It was a different matter as competition from overseas mounted. When design and production quality was neglected in favour of what the Japanese call "financial engineering" – the manipulation of cost without regard for quality – no amount of play with surface form could compensate for the lack of a holistic approach to design, in which every detail mattered. An example of what can be achieved by placing design and quality at the core of corporate strategy is the story of Chrysler Corporation in the last two decades, which recovered from the brink of extinction to a remarkable revival in the 1990s.

The story of how industrial design emerged and has subsequently developed in the United States has been substantially dependent at all stages upon the decisions and attitudes of managers and shareholders, and in the last analysis, in general terms, upon the American public's attitudes to design. As an activity it is intertwined with the general culture of any society and age and can only successfully contribute to the extent it is understood and harnessed in ways that realise its potential. In that sense, the final statement of George Nelson's Fortune article of 1934 is still profoundly relevant today: "Designers will not cure our industrial ills, for our ills lie deeper than design." [11] The potential of design to contribute to solutions, however, still remains unrealised on many levels.

1 Elizabeth Hoyt: Consumption in our Society. New York: McGrawHill, 1938, based on U.S. Bureau of the Census, Biennial Census of Manufactures, 1935, page 18. / 2 "Both Fish and Fowl." Fortune, February 1934, page 98. / 3 "Bulletin of The Carnegie Institute of Technology, 1933-34", Pittsburgh, PA, page 79. / 4 Business Week, May 1936. / 5 Harold Van Doren: Industrial Design - A Practical Guide. New York: McGraw-Hill, page 16. / 6 Typescript announcement document in Deskey collection, Cooper-Hewitt Museum, New York. / 7 Raymond Loewy: "Industrial Design Gives More Than A New Look: Knowing What you Need Comes First." The Iron Age: The National Metalworking Weekly, May 9, 1957. / 8 "Designers: Men Who Sell Change." Business Week, April 12, 1958. / 9 Donald Deskey: "Foreign Imports will buy more U.S. counsel on U.S. marketing." Printers Ink, January 1, 1960. / 10 David Halberstam: The Reckoning. New York: William Morrow and Co. Inc., 1986, page 210. / 11 "Both Fish and Fowl." Fortune, February, 1934, page 98.

'Model No.14' designed by Michael Thonet, Vienna 1859

Defining Design in the 20th Century

by Conway Lloyd Morgan

Conway Lloyd Morgan is a freelance journalist and lives in London. He is the editor and leading author of the "avedition rockets" series. As a connoisseur of the international design and architecture scene, he has published books on Philippe Starck, Marc Newson and Jean Nouvel. He writes regularly for 'Graphics International' and was the editor of the 'International Design Yearbook' from 1995 to 1997. He is now the editor of the trade fair design publication "Jahrbuch Messedesign".

It's a sobering thought that the product most widely known in the world by its designer's name was sketched in a military hospital in 1942: the designer never earned any royalties on the product, some 70 million of which have since been manufactured, but he did get the Stalin Prize, First Class. His name? Mikhail Timofevitch Kalashnikov. Even American rednecks or Zimbabwean rebels would recognise that name. Chappelon and Mitchell, Nizzoli and Race, Sason and Gugelhoff would leave them blank, even though they perhaps know about trains and planes, sewing machines and seating, cars and radios.

The twentieth century has been termed the century of design: if this is to have any sense it has to account for the terrorist's weapon of choice as well as the ideals of the Bauhaus and the iconoclastic fun of Memphis. The history of design in the twentieth century only has real validity if it can be read alongside the social, political and economic account of the time, and the two integrated in some way. There are some obvious points of contact: the Russian Futurists' attempts to redesign the world into a worker's uniform were a direct response to political change, and Barthes assured us that the Citroen DS was the ultimate emblem of bourgeois culture. One can read into the frivolity of Art Deco, relief at surviving the First World War; into the hedonism of 1960s Pop culture, flight from nuclear megadeath, and for post-modernism, read post-perestroika. One could further draw subtle connections between improvements in the design of healthcare products and the public health service changes widespread in Europe in the 1950s, and tie the development of signage systems generally to the rise in private motoring. One might cite the attempt by some European car makers in the 1950s to imitate American designs, but was their failure to succeed a reflection of Europe's lapse in understanding America's growing hegemony? Are these just coincidences or subtle indicators of some underlying causality?

One of the most influential books on 20th century design is Niklaus Pevsner's 'Pioneers of Modern Design'. It was first published at a time (1936)

'Panton chair' designed by Verner Panton, 1968

Radio-Phono-Combination SK4, 'Phonosuper' designed by Hans Gugelot and Dieter Rams, Braun 1956

when, it could be argued, America was making strong claims to be seen as the modern state, as opposed to fractured and imperial Europe. Pevsner makes an elegant claim for modernism, in design, to have impeccably liberal and European roots, and he presents a Darwinian model of design as evolving through principles and aesthetics, even creating a tree of development that conveniently puts down models of design he disapproves of, as dead ends. Thirty years later, while the deconstructivists were questioning the validity in art and literature of the very models that Pevsner used, Jean Baudrillard began publishing the series of books on the semiotics of the modern world that would argue that consumer society was a completely new type of society that could and must be read through its visible signs – its products and designs.

Thirty years or so further on, and we realise that neither Pevsner's academic rectitude nor Baudrillard's neo-Marxist eagerness provide a complete answer. The former was right to draw our attention to the continuing belief that design was a process of principle as well as aesthetics, the latter was correct in insisting that modern Western society is radically different from past societies, and consumer goods are a key element in that difference. But Pevsner was wrong to divorce design from its social context, and Baudrillard's rhetoric evades the necessary comparisons between Marxist definitions of capitalism and the contemporary world. Traditional design history insists that the Bauhaus, for example, had a leading role in developing the role of the designer, but as John Heskett has long pointed out, the influence of the Bauhaus lies more in its subsequent reputation than its actual achievements. Indeed Heskett's 1980 book, Industrial Design, did much to bring design back into a social, industrial and economic context, and so banish the invalid art-historical model. The social approach enables us to discern in the new industries, particularly for houseware and electrical goods, both before and after the Second World War, a need for new forms not only to encase new products, but also, to make them comprehensible and so useful to consumers. The stylistic disguises of the 19th century were no longer appropriate, aesthetically or commercially, and Modernism in art, architecture and literature offered an alternative approach, which already had engaged the interest of both designers and consumers.

What, then, does this internal history of design tell us? One immediately evident conclusion is that if the 20th century was perhaps not the century of design, it certainly was the century of the designer. The profession of designer evolved during that time from an artisan and artistic role into a new kind of mediator, concerned no longer just with decoration or even with form, but with creating meaning. This was a global process, not just a European one, but the European aspect was in several ways different from the American, and deserves independent consideration, though the two approaches evidently affected each other. Take the situation after the Second World War. Europe was devastated, physically and politically. In Germany and Italy, and to a lesser extent in France, design became a way of marking a break with the immediate past: one has only to look at the early work of Sottsass and Bellini, or of Dieter Rams, to see design as the vocabulary of a new social message. In Britain the victory of the left in post-War elections led to a new social awareness in housing and healthcare that fed through into design as well. This process in Europe was part of a wider activity in which not just designers, but politicians and industrialists, educators and journalists all played a part.

Through the 1960s, 1970s and 1980s the expansion in the range of consumer goods (televisions, telephones, kitchen appliances, hi-fi systems) created new challenges of product semantics, and the general increase in living standards across Western Europe created opportunities for designers to express their ideas in all kinds of ways, from the gritty to the genteel and the minimal to the mad. The apparent ending of the Cold War relaxed the moral grip of Modernism, and the growth in information technologies and control systems freed many areas of design from mechanical constraints, so offering new styling options. The rise of the design superstar, in the 1990s – personified of course by Philippe Starck – coincided with an increased appreciation in the media and in manufacturing

'Mercedes SL Roadster' by DaimlerChrysler, 1957, 1974, 2001

industry of the importance of design. The example of Swatch, where design, directed by Alessandro Mendini, enabled a whole industry to win back a lost market, is only one of many occasions when design has changed a company's fortunes. Design is now often talked of as the 'third leg' of modern manufacturing business, alongside marketing and production. Almost as a consequence, as Stephen Bayley once pointed out, the term designer became almost debased, much as 'executive' had a couple of decades before. If a product was called 'designer', it probably meant that the manufacturer could not think of anything better to call it. It is strange to consider how few 'designer' products carried a designer's name as well!

If, at the end of the century of the designer, the word designer means either a darling of the lifestyle press or a dubious label, where does that leave design? Somewhere in between, I would submit, and as such, in a mature position. For design was not only born in the 20th century, it grew up then as well. This accounts for the diversity of design as we see it around us – minimal to hi-tech, organic to surreal, monochrome to multicoloured – and the difficulty of creating a general definition or theory to fit it. One can construct endless design alphabets from AEG to Zanotta, from Aalto to Zwart, from Aicher to Zapf, from Bauhaus to Ulm, from Teddy Baumann to Tom Wolfe, or from Castiglione to Vitra, or from Droog to Utility, or from Formica to Philips, from Formalism to Virtuality: alphabets of designers, manufacturers, ideas. But that would be only to describe design, not define it. Perhaps design, by its very diversity, is moving beyond simple definitions. Perhaps design is now so firmly embedded in the fabric of society that we cannot usefully define it as a whole, but need to look at the parts, explore the structure and its implications. For design has not lost its future by being involved in the everyday: talk to Mendini, to Nouvel, to Starck, to Lovegrove, to Maurer and the visionary spirit, in many different guises, is still there. Design history and design theory are not over. We are stuck with our designers: and a good thing too. They are interesting, colourful, challenging people, and the world is the richer for having them: even if one of them was called Kalashnikov.

Development of Industrial Design in Asia

By Singanapalli Balaram and Darlie O. Koshy

Singanapalli Balaram is an educator, writer and Principal Designer at the National Institute of Design. He is presently Chairperson of the Knowledge Management Centre as well as Head of the Interdisciplinary Design Studies. His publications include "Thinking Design" book and major chapters in 'Britannica Encyclopedia Asia', 'Universal Design Hand Book', 'The Idea of Design' and 'Universal Design: 17 ways of Thinking and Teaching'. He serves on the advisory board of "Design Issues, MIT Press, USA, the Board of Governors of National Institute of Fashion Technology and Centre for Environmental Planning & Technology.

Dr. Darly O. Koshy is Executive Director and ex-officio member of the Governing Council, the National Institute of Design, India. He holds a Doctorate in Management from IIT and is a recipient of the UNDP Fellowship. He is on the Boards of various leading organisations in the Public and Private Sectors in India. He is an internationally known author, speaker, academician and consultant with twenty-four years of professional experience in the fields of textile and fashion.

World history is often criticised for its eurocentricity while Asia has been rather conspicuous by its absence. This is even more so in the case of design history. Even in the twenty-first century which is termed the "information age", one is not likely to find enough information on the design scene in Asian countries with the sole exception of Japan. One of the many contributing reasons is the region's preoccupation with survival needs in the process of development. The other, is the image of design which projected itself as Raymond Loewy's superficial streamlining, Louis Sullivan's self-conscious form following function, the rebellious extravaganza of the Memphis group, or the creations of the enfant terrible of design, Philippe Starck. Around the late 1950s and early 1960s, Asian leaders did recognise the significance of design along with management and technology as catalysts in the industrialisation process. Many design and technology institutions were founded and infrastructures were established. However, the realisation of the full potential of design did not occur until the winds of globalisation began to blow in the late eighties and early nineties. There has been a 20-30 year hiatus, and Asia is now eager to bridge the gap in the fastest possible manner. Asia's race for development has recently been faster than in all the other regions of the world. Not surprisingly, the future of global enterprise is expected to depend significantly on the present rate of rapid modernisation in the Asian countries.

Asia, however, is not a unified entity. It has more diversities than commonalities. It is a vast region covering diverse cultures and ethnicities, different national histories and unique deep-rooted cultures. In terms of the size of human population alone, Asia outweighs the rest of the world. With the rapid economic development in recent years, the countries of Asia have developed a relationship of interdependence and mutual influence on each other's society and culture. This relationship is accelerated by information technology and the internet revolution.

A glimpse of the design developments in some of the Asian countries reveals that the countries which were turning to the west in the 20th century for help and leadership are now turning towards each other for mutual collaboration because they are now more conscious of their

Sony 'NM-E3 Network Walkman' by Sony Design Center, Sony Corporation, 2001

cultural identities, developmental similarities and strengths. The design profession has finally started to show signs of maturity. The economic, social and cultural realities of many Asian countries with their sizeable chunks of population faced with poverty, illiteracy and lack of infrastructure call for attitudinal checks on the part of the fashioners of the new world, and for them to be sensitive and responsive to the needs of people, conditioned by their social, economic, cultural and environmental demands, which are varied and specific to the individual regional conditions. Design must be culturally relevant and acceptable to different communities within nation states. Design is an important step in the process of transition. When technologies change at a rapid pace and the resulting aspirations create an imbalance in social and cultural patterns, the design process can be harnessed to create harmony between technology, cultures and the environment. Design has the capacity to humanise technology and harmonise cultural diversity. Designers and design educators have an added responsibility, especially in Asian countries, to create appropriate products and services which assist in the pursuit of economic prosperity, social transformation and environmental and cultural harmony.

A glimpse of the developments in Asian design reveals the urge to 'design for need' while responding to 'design for desire'. This is a consistent pattern in almost all Asian countries. Singapore's Changi Airport is a visual metaphor of the country and its design situation – conspicuously clean, high tech and efficient, it speaks for the country's aspiration of a technological future. But its aesthetics are self-conscious and imposed. Government control is evident everywhere in the city. Singapore recognised the difference design can make through trade fairs abroad and in 1984 included design promotion as an important activity of the Singapore Trade Development Board. The board, following a previous programme of the Design Council in the UK, gives financial support to first clients by paying up 75% of the design fee. Besides, the government encourages and helps overseas design firms and manufacturers to design products locally. As Singapore is a trading port, change by design is essential and the government is persevering with its implementation. In 1990, more than a decade ago, Singapore started a series of biennial international design forums, which have become very popular. The forums themselves are designed events with thoughtfully selected 'design stars' as speakers and beautiful venues with space for overseas design exhibitions. In the same year, Singapore launched the 'Young Designers Award" for students aged between 13 and 17 to make the young aware of design and to encourage them to get interested in design. This is indeed a laudable initiative because design can flourish only in a design-educated society. Singapore is trying to build up an indigenous design capability on the one hand, while trying to preserve its cultural identity on the other. But before preserving cultural identity, one first needs to discover it, because Singapore's heritage is a mix of ethnic Chinese, Malays and Indians, in that order. It may not be easy, but the search is on.

Malaysia's geographical location between the Indian Ocean and the South China Sea is perhaps a factor in its history of continual influences of the west as well as the east. After its independence from Britain in 1957, the country's development process accelerated and it is considered today as one of the most attractive destinations in Asia for investment. The key role design can play in industrial development was recognised soon after its independence, and by 1971, a new economic policy was introduced to encourage local manufacturers to use design as a creative tool in the application of new technology to reduce the nation's dependence on imported products. By the 1990s, Malaysia succeeded in becoming a manufactured product exporter, thus superseding its earlier status as a commodity exporter. Formal design education in Malaysia started in the late 1960s with teachers imported from neighbouring Thailand and Australia. It adopted the British model of design education. Today, Malaysia is conscious of the need to establish its own design identity. The government is allocating finances and making policies to encourage local design and local brands. In 1994 the Malaysia Design Council was established under the Department of Science and Technology for design promotion and design awareness. The council recognises outstanding designs by conferring the good design mark award for products and services. In spite of all these efforts, the Malaysian industry still plays it safe and

prefers to emulate the catalogues brought in from the west, rather than venting into indigenous products through innovation. Addressing this issue is the surest way for Malaysia to establish its identity in the globalised future.

In 1958, the eminent Charles Eames projected 'Iota', the traditional Indian vessel, as an inspiring example for the emerging Indian design profession to follow. India's design story is quite similar to that of other colonised countries, except for its long history of over 5000 years of artistic sensibility and aesthetic explorations of design in various forms. In 1961, professional design training commenced in India with the establishment of India's first multidisciplinary design school, the National Institute of Design (NID) at Ahmedabad. The founders studied the world's best design schools, such as the Bauhaus, HfG Ulm, Royal College of Art and die Allgemeine Gewerbeschule, taking an eclectic view to evolve their own kind of design education. As few other design schools followed suit, the impact of design on Indian industries has been inadequate. While, on the one hand, the excellence of design education produced professionals of international standard, on the other hand, design in India badly lacked promotional support.

After over four decades of design, India neither has a design council nor a design policy which can catapult Indian design to its deserved place in the country's economic progress and social development. Global competition, a result of liberalisation, did however force a few Indian industries to pursue innovation and indigenous design, but they remain just a handful of exceptions. The problem is aggravated by the complexity of Indian production, which is marked by the simultaneous presence of large scale, small scale, craft, and cottage activity. Promotional efforts led by institutions and individuals have been sporadic and could not be sustained. A major initiative was the first UNIDO-ICSID meeting on 'Design for Development' (1979), which led to the most significant 'Ahmedabad Declaration' signed by 37 countries. The Golden Eye project of the eighties is another innovative design experiment, which focused on a revival of the Indian craft industry. (It can certainly be called an industry, being a source of employment for 23 million people.) Star designers such as Ettore Sottsass, Mario Bellini, Milton Glaser, Ivan Chermayeff and Frei Otto were invited to India to work with Indian master craftsmen and design unique craft products. Festivals of India of the 1980's also brought about a design revival in the craft sector. In this regard, the setting up of the techno-design interface group in 2001 by the government of India's Department of Science and Technology, the collaborative efforts of the Governing Council, the National Institute of Design, with the confederation of Indian industry in having annual design summits since 2001 and the establishment of India's first permanent design display centre, Showcase Design, by NID-ITPO augur well for design, initiating a design movement in the country.

Korea is a country which in the past used to function as a conduit for Chinese, Mongol and Japanese influences. Now, while it cannot help admiring and emulating Japan for its economic and commercial progress, it also would like to be distinct from Japan, which had been its invader from 1910 to 1945. Korea's economy operates through "chaebols", the massive conglomerates. The chaebols initially grew by imitating the zaibatsu (giant corporations) of Japan, and copying Japanese and German products. Now they are looking for distinction and a Korean identity. This identity is important for Korean people and nowadays, one finds no foreign vehicles on the Korean streets, but only Korea's own Hyundais or Daewoos. While its old guard designers were educated in Korean schools, often by Japanese teachers, the young generation is educated in the west and acutely aware of the international developments in technology and design. The Korean government took a direct interest in design as a tool for economic prosperity and rapid industrialisation, and thus, the first five-year plan for industrial promotion,1993-97, resulted in significant growth among designers and design firms. The economic crisis of 1997 further emphasised the need for an accelerated design strategy. The second five-year plan included design and infrastructure provision, and public awareness started at the national level. Korea has set a target to elevate the quality of Korean design to 80-90% of that of the advanced countries. In 2001 Korea set up one of the world's largest design centres, whose com-

'Samsung 241 MP TFT-LCD', television set by Samsung Electronics, 2002

prehensive facilities include a design innovation centre and a business incubator, together with large convention and exhibition halls. It is not surprising, then, that despite the country's size, thousands of students are enrolled annually in design programmes and Korea's design competitiveness worries even developed countries.

Despite the terrible losses sustained in 1945 at the end of Second World War, Japan has risen to strength in design, and manufacturing and as a trading power, and its national economy excels in the world today. It has been a phenomenal achievement in such a short time. Japan occupies a unique position in the world in applying its traditional, strictly disciplined work culture to modern day manufacture and marketing strategies. Japan began its industrialisation process by copying the best selling products from abroad and exporting them at unbeatable prices. It soon passed this phase and sought to find its distinctive character on the global market. Japan is the first industrialised country in Asia. Under its Ministry of Trade & Industry, it established the good design 'G' mark as early as in 1957, followed by the Japan Industrial Promotion Organisation in 1969 and the Japan Design Foundation in 1981. Its activities include constant information exchange, regular design competitions and design promotion through exhibitions and conferences. In the 1970 World Exhibition held at Osaka, the theme was 'Design for every being'. In most cases, invention strongly dominates Japanese designs. Japanese products, from Toyota's automobiles to Sony's Walkman, are distinguished by their miniaturised grace, addressing the reality of an ever-present squeeze on domestic space. But recently, a trend towards larger products has become noticeable in Japanese designs, and perhaps largeness is seen as a metaphor of affluence, which can be attributed to the changed values of a new generation. Japan is always keen on its international presence. The head of the GK Design firm, Kenji Ekuan, was president of ICSID in the mid seventies. Japan is truly globalised today, considering that more than half of its corporate identity programmes are performed by foreign designers such as Saul Bass for Minolta, or Chermanyeff and Geismar for Nissan. The phrase "local at home and global outside of it" neatly summarises the Japanese design attitude.

Thailand supports the preservation of the Thai culture through education, research, animation and development, in order that it may serve as an important tool for solving problems encountered in the conduct of individual life, for the development of social, economic and political progress, and for the strengthening of national sovereignty. The role of industrial design in this regard is well accepted in Thailand. Leading universities offer design as part of their regular educational programmes and, as a part of its policy to promote the development of product design for export and to support Thai designers the Department of Export Promotion organises design contests and conferences through its Product Development Centre.

Australia is a multicultural country, which established the Industrial Design Council of Australia in 1958 with the aim of promoting design and improving the quality of Australian manufactured products. In 1975, with the creation of a Commonwealth Statutory Authority under the Australian Council Act, Australian design received a further impetus. Considering education and awareness as key aspects in the progress of industry and the economy, Australia established design education in art schools following the British model. The Design Institute of Australia was founded in 1958 to serve professional designers practising as private consultants or in-house designers. The institute acts like a trade association and maintains standards of professional competence and ethical conduct among Australian designers. In 1984, the institute established national awards for both professional and student designers including an exhibition of winning entries. Australia believes in the concept of well designed products to satisfy the criteria of commercial visibility, technical competency and human factors, which include aesthetic, ergonomic, environmental and economic considerations. The council established 'The Australian Design Award' in 1977 as the vehicle to provide recognition for well designed products. It recognised that increased ownership by Australian industry of the designs of the products it makes, is a fundamental principle for Australian industry's growth, replacing the earlier and easier copying or licensing designs from other countries. A variety of initiatives were started,

'Toyota RSC' Roadster designed Toyota Motor Corpration, 2001

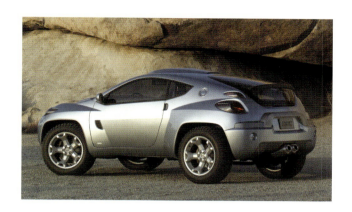

and these may well serve as models for other countries. These include an advisory service in design, training courses in product development, online design data and grants for Australian designers to participate in international design conferences.

While reviewing the design scene in Asia, China is worthy of special mention. China, – the 'waking dragon' – is clearly a focus for world attention. A country where one quarter of the earth's population resides is keen on competing worldwide, not just in China and Asia. By organising its enormous labour force, China is already producing quality products at incredibly cheap prices. Chinese design educators are presently concerned about the marketability, sustainability, aesthetics and function of products. The world's most powerful country, the USA, wishes to collaborate with China. In the words of IDSA (Industrial Designers Society of America) education committee chairman Jim Kaufman, "When they (the Chinese) move from a manufacturing source to a product development position, they will truly have a product design presence in the world". China has recently set up a Design Brand and Brand Policy Division to put a special focus on design and the establishment of brands.

The Asian countries are still agrarian at their core, though many of the countries are rapidly industrialising. China, India, Thailand, the Philippines, Malaysia, Pakistan or Sri Lanka are no different from each other in this regard. The urge to use design intervention to hasten industrial progress and economic prosperity is present in varying degrees in all the Asian countries. The south-east Asian tigers and other developing countries in Asia are increasingly using the power of design to increase their per capita GNP and unit value realisation of products by industry, and most importantly, to project their national cultures and identities. The true test of Asian design will, however, lie in their ability to transform from the local to the global, while addressing both the challenges concerning 'design for need' and 'design for desire' and whilst managing the diversity the region embodies.

COMPANIES

Tom Ahlström, Hans Ehrich

Sweden

A&E Design AB

Rehnsgatan 11
S-11357 Stockholm
Tel. +46 8 673 01 59
Fax +46 8 673 49 21
info@aedesign.se
www.aedesign.se

A&E Design

A&E Design is Tom Ahlström and Hans Ehrich. They have won the "Excellent Swedish Design Award" 14 times, and five times the prestigious international "red dot award", three of those being in the "best of the best" category for unusual and outstanding product design. Over 300 products now bear the stamp of Tom Ahlström and Hans Ehrich, making A&E Design without a doubt one of the leading service providers for industrial design in Sweden.

Hans Ehrich, who is now regarded as the grand seigneur of Swedish product design, studied design and metalwork at the Konstfackskolan in Stockholm, as did his partner Tom Ahlström, before they opened their design studio together in 1968. With their penchant for practical applications and elegant solutions, they have focused their attention not only on product design for the handicapped, but also and in particular on the development of new applications for plastics. As a result, Hans Ehrich and Tom Ahlström have designed a large number of unobtrusive but effective products and left their unmistakable mark on the system of everyday objects and our quotidian culture. "They strive for an optimum balance between aesthetics, function and the needs of the market", as they themselves repeatedly emphasise. It is not surprising, therefore, that around 20 percent of all projects at A&E Design are concerned with the further development of their own product designs. Together with innovation in design, therefore, A&E attaches importance to the consistent optimisation and improvement of existing products.

In that context, many of the products evoke formal associations with Italian design in the mind of the observer, and the two inseparable designers Hans Ehrich and Tom Ahlström would never deny that they were influenced above all in their work by Joe Colombo. In 1970, the two designers added a workshop to their A&E Design studio, in order to develop carefully constructed models and prototypes, together with detailed ergonomic products. In this way their meticulousness, their detailed studies and their specific knowledge are transformed into maximum benefit for the user. These achievements were honoured in 1987 with the "Designer of the Year" award.

Stockholm II: Chairs or stools are without a doubt highly mobile objects, but there are still certain limits to their transport. Stockholm II is the first folding stool specifically for visitors to museums and exhibitions. It is a lightweight folding stool weighing 1.75 kg. The frame is made from curved, powder coated aluminium tubes, and the joint of die cast aluminium. The seat consists of glass fibre reinforced plastic fabric and can be replaced if necessary quite simply.

The specially designed transport trolley accommodates twenty stools and, with its four revolving castors, two of which are fitted with brakes, it can easily be moved to wherever temporary seating is required. In addition there is a wall mounting for five stools. The folding stool is not of course restricted to use in museums or exhibitions. It can be of assistance wherever there is an unexpected surge of people: at small cinemas, spontaneous gatherings, at parties or garden fetes.

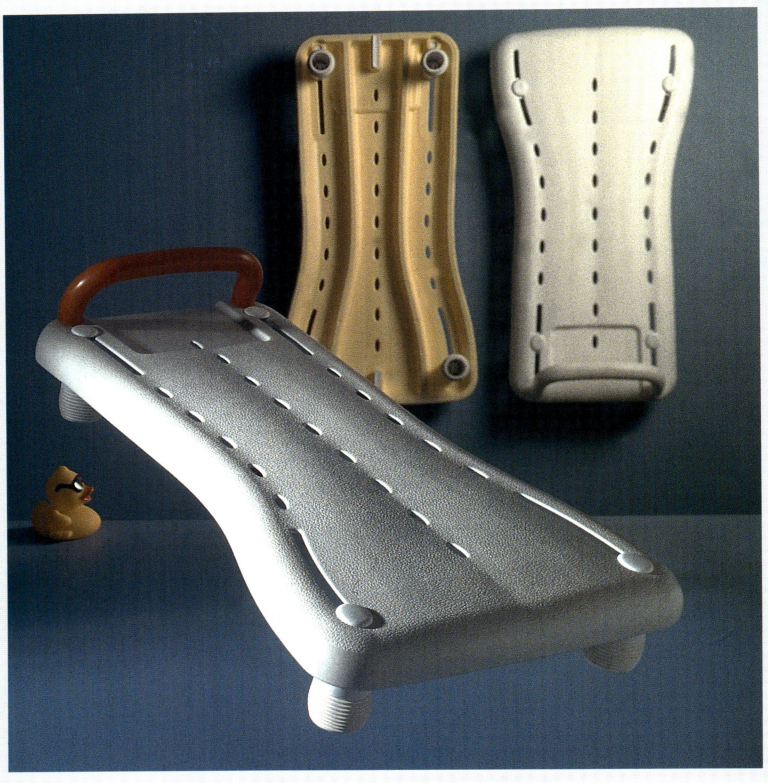

Fresh Plastic Bath Board. After a bath or shower, you feel fresh and clean. The feeling of harmony with one's own body is rapidly restored in this highly private cleaning ceremony. Not for the elderly or ill: they are often unable to get into the bath or shower alone. The nursing staff are confronted with a multitude of problems. In the design of the Fresh bath board, the function and form follow the criteria of care, safety and maximum comfort for the bather. It is made of polypropylene, and has an ergonomically soft and round shape. Four powerful edge stops with rubber friction surfaces ensure that the board rests firmly in the bath. The bather therefore feels safe and comfortable.

The bath board has a broad seating area at the front end, making it easier for the bather to run round or move sideways. The surface, with a large number of openings, is designed to allow the water to flow off freely. Fresh has an anti-slip pattern, to make showering easier. At the rear end, there is a soap dish, and a comfortable handle can also be fitted there. With its corner-free design, the bath board is easy to clean and totally hygienic. It is manufactured by a highly specialized process, creating a recyclable plastic product with hermetically sealed, air-filled cavities. The Fresh bath board restores dignity to the elderly and infirm, and creates a new aesthetics of bathing.

Clean Shower Chair. Questions of ethics and aesthetics play a major role in design for people with handicaps. The Clean shower and toilet chair is such a product. The brief was to design a shower and toilet chair with improved handling both for the patient and for the nursing staff. In order to avoid the corrosion problems encountered with other toilet units, the frame is manufactured from a single, 4.3 m long, steel tube. The seat, back rest, arm rests and foot plate are manufactured from polypropylene. The selection of materials, shapes and surface finish ensure that the chair is dirt-repellent and easy to clean. The rear surfaces of theses parts are smooth, without corners and angles, and can therefore fulfil the highest demands for hygiene.

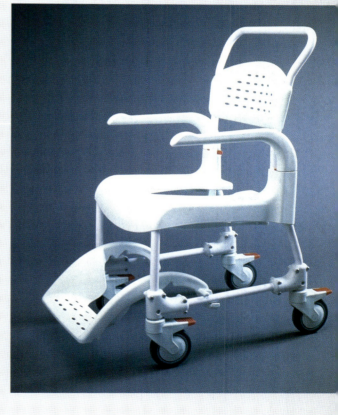

Germany

AEG

AEG Hausgeräte GmbH

Muggenhofer Straße 135
D-90429 Nürnberg
Tel. +49 911 323-0
Fax +49 911 323-1770
info@aeg-hausgeraete.de
www.aeg-hausgeraete.de

When the artist and architect Peter Behrens was engaged in 1907, the former "Allgemeine Elektricitäts-Gesellschaft" was the first industrial company in Germany to create the position of "artistic advisor", the person in the company responsible for corporate concepts and product design. Peter Behrens not only designed several buildings for AEG; company logos and a number of appliances also bore his designer signature. A remark made by Paul Jordan, at that time Chairman of the Board of Directors at AEG, shows just how significant product design already was for the company. In 1929, Jordan said to Peter Behrens: "Don't believe for one minute that an engineer, on buying a motor, will take it apart to examine it. Even he, as an expert, will base his purchase on appearance. A motor must look like a birthday present."

AEG has maintained this tradition, even after reconstruction. It recommenced operations in 1953 with the founding of the Head Office for Design, which was located in Frankfurt and was responsible for all AEG AG business areas. With the merger of AEG and Telefunken in 1968 the company formed its own group to design household appliances, which at that time was already located in Nuremberg. Hans Werner Friedlaender headed this group

AEG

until 1984, when he assumed the position of Corporate Identity Officer with AEG Hausgeräte AG, a spin-off of AEG-Telefunken AG since 1983. With the founding of AEG Hausgeräte AG, and under the composition proceedings of AEG AG in Frankfurt, the product design section was closed down and for the next two years, the agency frogdesign in Altensteig was engaged for designing purposes. Subsequent to this two-year period, the consultant in charge at frogdesign, Hans Strohmeier, left the company and joined AEG Hausgeräte AG. From 1987 to 1989 he was Acting Head of the Design Department at AEG, and he then became permanent head. When Electrolux took over AEG Hausgeräte in 1994, the design department was also integrated into the European company, and, besides being responsible for AEG, was from then on also responsible for the brand names Juno, Zanker and Therma, as well as for design projects of the Electrolux Group throughout Europe. The department is still headed by Hans Strohmeier today, who now holds the position of Design Director. He is also a member of the Electrolux Design Management Team Europe.

Throughout the changing history of the company, AEG household appliances have always been characterised by creativity and innovative design, proof of which is given by the number of international design awards which AEG products have received, particularly in the past few years. AEG household appliances are well known in Europe under product names like "Lavamat", "Favorit", "Competence", „Preference", "Santo" and "Arctis" as a synonym for high quality, ecology and design.

One Touch 715

France

Alcatel Mobile Phone

32, Avenue Kléber
92707 Colombes Cedex
Tel. +33 155 66 34 12
Fax +33 155 66 74 95
www.alcatel.com

Alcatel

The Alcatel company can trace its history back to 31 May 1898, when French engineer Pierre Azaria set up the Compagnie Generale d'Electricite (CGE). It adopted its present name in 1980. Alcatel designs, develops and builds innovative and competitive telecommunications products, and produces services to deliver any type of content, such as voice, data and multimedia, to any type of consumer, in more than 130 countries. With someone on the planet buying an Alcatel GSM phone every three seconds, the company's mobile phone division is currently among the biggest in the world.

Headquartered in Paris, Alcatel understands the importance of the alchemy between aesthetics and function. From concept communication devices of the future to mobile phones today, Alcatel's One Touch range is proving popular with everyone from impoverished students to globe-trotting businessmen.

One Touch 512

The design of Alcatel's mobile phones has been recognised by various institutions including the following:
Design Awards 2002 for One Touch 511 iF Design Award, Industrie Forum Design (Germany) / Observeur du Design, APCI (France)
Design Awards 2001 for One Touch 300-500-700 Observeur du Design, APCI (France) / iF Design Award, Industrie Forum Design (Germany)
Design Awards 1999 for One Touch Easy db Janus de l'Industrie, Institut Français du Design (France) / G-Mark, JIDPO (Japan) / Observeur du Design, APCI (France) / Red Dot for High Design Quality, Design Zentrum Nordrhein Westfalen (Germany)

In order to remain at the forefront of design and technology, Alcatel works with young designers because they are best positioned to determine what will be tomorrow's trends and thinking. The managers at Alcatel appreciate that design students are the professional designers of the future. With this in mind, Alcatel's design teams regularly invite students from schools all over the world to present their ideas for futuristic communication devices in general as well as mobile phones. The resulting concepts often exhibit a freshness and boldness in their creativity, encouraging thought rather than practical solutions – free from the doctrinaire considerations that may constrain many of Alcatel's practising designers.

The participating schools in this Alcatel sponsored design initiative include Shih Chien University, Taipei, Taiwan, Hong Kong University, Hong Kong, China, Ecole Nationale Superieur de Creation Industrielle, Paris, France, Strate College, Paris, France, and the Escola Superior de Disseny Elisava, Barcelona, Spain.

Germany

Blanco

Blanco GmbH + Co KG

Flehinger Str. 59
75038 Oberderdingen
Germany
Tel. +49 7045 44-0
Fax +49 7045 44-299
info@blanco.de
www.blanco.de

With a history of over 75 years, Blanco has become successfully established as a key supplier of kitchen technology, food service equipment and medical engineering products. The company is well diversified to face the future.

Today, Blanco has branches and production facilities in several countries around the world and is represented on all the relevant national markets. All the production facilities are state of the art. With the highly automated stainless steel sink plant in Sulzfeld the company has the most modern works of its kind in Europe, thus assuring the high quality of the Blanco brand.

Blanco's strategic position is based on innovative product policy and clear brand orientation. Design at Blanco revolves around people, with their communicative, aesthetic and ergonomic needs. The key to successful design is to be found in the synthesis between convincing functionality and attractive aesthetics. Blanco always backs innovation, and regards design as an instrument of differentiation and brand building. Many of the company's successful products have won design awards.

At Blanco, every new design is a fundamental process, starting with carefully thought-out and future-orientated concept developments. In the design of workplaces, the focus is on utility value and function, made apparent in a clear language of form. The designers and marketing specialists in the company attach importance to clean lines, appropriate and high quality materials, so as to emphasise the value of the products.

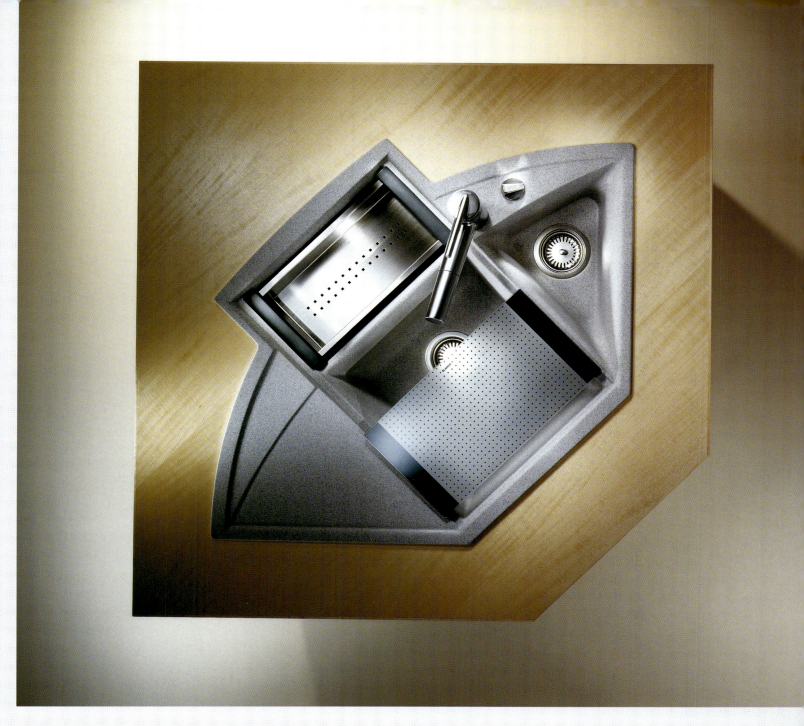

BLANCOAXIA The design of the sink unit centres on the granite look of the Silgranit® material used. The concept recalls traditional slop-stones. It is packed with practical features, extra large deep bowls and a large colander / strainer bowl.

Germany

**Burkhard Leitner
constructiv GmbH & Co.**

Blumenstraße 36
70182 Stuttgart
Tel. +49 711 255 88-0
Fax +49 711 255 88-11
info@burkhardtleitner.de
www.burkhardtleitner.de

Burkhardt Leitner constructiv

Founded in Stuttgart in 1993, Burkhard Leitner constructiv has evolved into one of the leading makers of modular architecture systems. With offices in Stuttgart and Berlin, the company develops and distributes exhibition, interior, display, shop and office systems. The team, which is now more than thirty strong, handles the architecture projects of an international clientele – from draft planning to system development. The systems are sold by a steadily expanding network of independent planning, service and sales partners worldwide. Part of the philosophy of Burkhard Leitner constructiv is that a company should be aware of both its social and cultural responsibilities, and therefore the business is actively engaged in promoting design and art. It takes part in design competitions or workshops for up- and-coming designers, and supports mainly young artists

with a non-profit gallery "Ausstellung im Kabinett" in Stuttgart. To incorporate art into everyday life, Burkhard Leitner constructiv commissions a wide variety of artists to redesign its company franking stamp every three months.

Design Awards 2001: Design Preis Schweiz (Switzerland) / Das Gute Stück, Deutscher Designer Club (Germany) / iF Design Award, Industrie Forum Design (Germany) / „Innovationspreis Architektur und Office – Möbel für Architekten", AIT, ABIT und Intelligente Architektur (Germany) / best selection: office design, Design Zentrum Nordrhein Westfalen (Germany)
Design Awards 2000: Focus Arbeitswelten, Internationaler Designpreis des Landes Baden-Württemberg (Germany) / Red Dot for the Highest Design Quality, Design Zentrum Nordrhein Westfalen (Germany)
Design Awards 1999 iF Exhibition Design Award in Gold, Industrie Forum Design (Germany) / Red Dot for the Highest Design Quality, Design Zentrum Nordrhein Westfalen (Germany)
Design Awards 1998: Bundespreis Produktdesign, Rat für Formgebung (Germany)
Design Awards 1997: Markterfolge, Internationaler Designpreis des Landes Baden-Württemberg (Germany) / Langlebigkeit, Internationaler Designpreis des Landes Baden-Württemberg (Germany) / Finalist of the European Design Prize (1997)
The Company's Clients include Audi, Bertelsmann, BMW, Bosch, brandeins, Brose, Bundestag, Carnegie-Mellon, Daimler-Chrysler, Condor, Datalogic, design report, Deutsches Museum, DLR, Dorint-Hotel, EGANA, Einhorn, EDF Electricité de France, Esselte, Fraunhofer Institut, fsb, Goldpfeil, Heinle, Wischer und Partner, Herman Miller, Hewlett Packard, HypoVereinsbank, International Design Center South Korea, Klett-Cotta, Lorenzini, Lufthansa, Mabeg, Nils Holger Moormann, Opel, Pepe Jeans, Plazamedia, Premiere, Rat für Formgebung, Regiolux, Schering, Schweiztourismus, SEB, Sony, Springer-Verlag, Staatsoper Stuttgart, Steelcase, Telekom, Toshiba, Toyota, Unifor, VW, Wellmann and Werndl.

USA

Crown

Crown Equipment Corporation

44 South Washington St.
New Bremen, OH 45869
Tel. +1 419 629-2311
Fax +1 419 629-3246
www.crown.com

Founded in 1945 by two brothers and still family-owned today, Crown is an international manufacturer and distributor of industrial lift equipment. Its global headquarters are in New Bremen, Ohio, in the United States. The European headquarters are in Munich, Germany, with manufacturing facilities in Germany, Ireland, and England. There are also manufacturing and sales facilities in Australia.

Crown's product line includes pallet trucks that can transport up to 3.6 tonnes (8000 lbs), standup and sitdown narrow aisle stacking trucks, sitdown counterbalance trucks, as well as operator-up order pickers and turret trucks that can lift up to 13.7 metres (45 feet). Key Crown innovations include the side stance operator compartment, awarded a Design of the Decade from IDSA, and the multi-function control handle, combining primary operator controls in one handle. Recent innovations include a sit-stand reach truck, and the Wave – a compact work assist vehicle that elevates both operator and load, allowing access up to 6.3 metres (13.4 feet).

Crown's design focus began in the early 1960s, when RichardsonSmith (now Fitch) was hired to design a new pallet truck, which won Crown's first design award. With the creation of an internal design centre in the early 1990s, design's role expanded to include strategic planning and involvement in all phases of product development. As Crown has grown, it has taken an increasingly global approach to product design. A new product may be designed in North America, manufactured in Europe, and sold in both markets. Crown Equipment Corporation spends a significant effort on design for two main reasons. Firstly, good design is good business. Whenever a lift truck goes down a warehouse aisle, an operator goes with it. Good design makes that operator's job easier, safer and more comfortable, and therefore more productive. Secondly, a good design organisation must continuously discover innovation and value for business. Crown design has been delivering such value for over 30 years. This focus on design has resulted in over 50 awards for Crown since 1965, not only for lift trucks, but also for design research, process, and consistency of language. The awards include the Red Dot for the Highest Design Quality from the Design Zentrum Nordrhein Westfalen, Outstanding Design, Best of Group, and Top Ten Awards from Industrie Forum Design, Design of the Decade and IDEA awards from the Industrial Designers Society of America, Design Distinction Awards from ID Magazine, and Good Design Awards from the Chicago Athenaeum, among others. With the materials handling industry changing more rapidly than ever, more and more manufacturers have begun to realise the value of design, which raises customer expectations significantly.

Crown Wave (Work Assist Vehicle) The Wave is a compact, highly manoeuvrable work assist vehicle designed to extend workers' capabilities by simultaneously transporting and elevating both operator and load, allowing access to shelves up to 6.3 metres (13.4 feet). The ability to travel securely while elevated greatly reduces operator fatigue. The load tray positions the work right where the operator needs it without blocking their view of the floor.

Crown SC 4000 The SC 4000 three-wheel sitdown counterbalanced lift truck combines innovative appearance, refined ergonomics and total manoeuvrability, establishing new paradigms in appearance while maintaining its identity as a Crown product. It is perfect for loading and unloading pallets on busy shipping docks, in tractor trailers and in aisles.

Germany/USA

DaimlerChrysler

DaimlerChrysler AG

DaimlerChrysler AG
70546 Stuttgart
Tel. +49 711 17-0
Fax +49 711 17-940 22
www.daimlerchrysler.com

DaimlerChrysler
Corporation, USA
Auburn Hills, Michigan,
MI 48326-2766
Tel. +1 248 576-57 41
Fax +1 248 576-47 42

For almost a year, from December 2000 to September 2001, the Mercedes-Benz brand has been celebrating its 100th anniversary under the slogan "The Story of Passion". Over 500 individual events, ranging from shows and trial driving presentations, to new model premieres and exhibitions, have formed the backdrop for reliving dramatic, amusing, exciting and sometimes unbelievable moments from the brand's history. The "Story of Passion" reached its pinnacle at 2001 IAA, gloriously culminating in the world premiere of the new SL-Class, the embodiment of automotive passion in its purest form.

During the the last year, Mercedes-Benz has provided many different insights, highlighting the fact that every one of the brand's successes has been achieved thanks to people with a passion for cars. The Mercedes-Benz story is a story about people who have achieved and still achieve a great deal. The same was true more than 100 years ago when the Daimler-Motoren-Gesellschaft company started using the name Mercedes for its vehicles. The new cars – ordered from Daimler-Motoren-Gesellschaft in 1900 by the Austrian diplomat and keen amateur racing driver Emil Jellinek – had to be light, fast and attractive. It was in one of these cars that he won at the racing week in Nice the year after. Such was his enthusiasm that he named the first modern car after his daughter Mercédès. Since then, the little girl's name has become one of the most famous brand names on every continent, standing for the power of innovation, technical perfection and the very highest quality standards.

The "Story of Passion" met with an extraordinary response as soon as it was "published" at a big press conference last December. The international media were keen to find out about the Mercedes-Benz brand, the founding fathers, the constructors, the customers, the racing drivers, the inventors, the safety experts, the designers and those researching the future of the automobile.

Mercedes SL: No other model captures the sentiment of the Mercedes "Story of Passion" slogan quite as aptly as the new SL Class. Like the forefather of this model series, the legendary 1954 300 SL, the new Roadster emphasises, among its many typical Mercedes qualities, one theme above all others: the dynamic sports car experience.

Two model versions were making their public debut at the Stuttgart-based car manufacturer's stand at the IAA: the SL 500 with its 225-kW/306-hp V8 engine and the SL 55 AMG, which has a newly developed supercharged engine, delivering an output of 350kW/476 hp and a maximum torque of 700 Nm from 2650 rpm – new record values in the current Mercedes-Benz car range. The new SL 55 AMG accelerates from 0 to 100 km/h in just 4.7 seconds.

Both SL Class models have a unique and impressive package of cutting-edge dynamic handling control systems, unrivalled by any other series-produced car in the world. It consists of the new electrohydraulic brake system, Sensotronic Brake Control (SBC), the Active Body Control system (ABC) and Electronic Stability Control ESP®. The optimum interaction of these systems ensures that the SL Class offers a very high degree of ride safety and outstanding handling.

Further high-tech innovations which come as standard in the new SL Class models include the vario-roof, which transforms the Roadster into a watertight Coupé in 16 seconds, the state-of-the-art lightweight body with its aluminium add-on parts and exemplary aerodynamics (cd value 0.29 in the SL 500), the sensor-controlled automatic climate control system and an adaptive drive system which automatically adapts to the driver's personal driving style. A new type of head/thorax sidebag in the doors, two-stage airbags for driver and passenger, newly developed integral seats and the automatic, sensor-controlled roll-over bars perfect the standard occupant protection on board of the new Mercedes Roadster.

Design philosophy: The Mercedes-Benz marque is the oldest, and at the same time the most famous automobile brand in the world. For the design of Mercedes-Benz vehicles, this has always entailed a responsibility to continue the tradition of the marque, even if of course the design of a new vehicle is per se a future-orientated act.

This influence resulted in an evolutionary development process right from the start, ensuring that every Mercedes can clearly be recognised as a member of the same family as its predecessors and the other models currently available. This is the basis of a pronounced product identity, leading to a long-term preservation of value. The design premises are however also subject to developments in the technical and social dimensions. In spite of the introduction of a host of design innovations, it has remained clear that there should be no radical break with tradition and therefore no irreparable loss of identity.

There are three fundamental statements:
  A Mercedes must always look like a Mercedes!
  It should symbolise all the values which a Mercedes has and which the customer expects of it.
  The design should comprise a maximum of innovation while respecting the tradition of the marque.

The Mercedes-Benz brand has progressed, and no longer stands exclusively for absolutely top of the range vehicles. The product offensive of recent years has created new concepts for new target groups. New concepts demand new forms of expression. Nevertheless, it is clear that the customers still want to have a Mercedes – and all the values associated with it.

Vaneo: new and innovative mini-MPV makes its first public appearance. Intelligent, multifunctional and family-friendly – the watchwords of the new Vaneo mini-MPV which is being presented to the public for the first time at the IAA 2001. With its space-saving sandwich construction, the 4.20-metre-long five-door vehicle realises a pioneering dimensional concept, which dedicates 65 to 70 percent of the on-board capacity to the passengers or luggage compartment. The Mercedes-Benz Vaneo delivers the capacity of a mini-MPV within the dimensions of a compact saloon.

There is room on board of this star mini-MPV for five adults and two children or up to 3000 litres of luggage. Young families, leisure-oriented couples, one-person households and so-called mixed users now have a tailor-made Mercedes-Benz for their needs – one which also acts as a benchmark in its class in terms of safety, thanks to four airbags, ABS, Brake Assist, ESP® and four belt tensioners. The three equipment lines, TREND, FAMILY and AMBIENTE, and the innovative additional packages, SNOW, SURF, BIKE, DOG and CARRY, together with three petrol engines and two diesel engines, allow plenty of scope for individualisation.

Germany

Duravit

Duravit AG

Werder Strasse 36
78132 Hornberg
Tel. +49 78331 70-0
Fax +49 78331 70-289
duravit@duravit.de
www.duravit.de

The history of the Duravit company began in Hornberg 184 years ago, when Georg Friedrich Horn established a small factory which was initially concerned with the production of stoneware crockery. "Sanitary washing articles" first went into production in Hornberg at the beginning of the 19th century. Since 1960, the Duravit brand has been a guarantee of quality from the Black Forest.

The company's manufacturing capacity has since undergone systematic expansion through the establishment of additional production plants in Bischwiller (France), Meissen (eastern Germany), Cairo (Egypt) and Istanbul (Turkey). Duravit established a successful second line of business when its bathroom furniture production plant in Schenkenzell (near Hornberg) went into operation almost 10 years ago. In its efforts to supply a genuinely comprehensive range, Duravit accords priority to ensuring variety in its range in a manner which is virtually unparalleled on the sanitaryware market. From basic forms to design bathrooms from Philippe Starck, Michael Graves, Massimo Iosa Ghini, Sieger Design or Norman Foster – Duravit covers all possible budgets and lifestyles.

The broad spectrum embraced by Duravit's range is subject to continual expansion. International marketing efforts have also been stepped up systematically in recent years, not only with regard to the necessary increase in personnel, but also in terms of adaptations to the range. Duravit's forward-looking strategies have seen the company develop above all on international markets: Numerous marketing companies and agencies in Europe, the USA, Middle East and Far East are contributing to the growth in foreign business.

There can be no doubt that design has also been instrumental to the company's international success – not least from the leading international designers who work for the company such as Sieger Design, Philippe Starck, Phoenix Product Design, Michael Graves, Massimo Iosa Ghini or Lord Foster. These have all long been established as absolute authorities in matters of bathroom design. This leading status imposes high standards on the form, colouring and functions of Duravit products. And these exacting standards have inspired the designers to great success – as confirmed by numerous awards from international design juries.

Philippe Starck Edition 1: With his bathroom range, Philippe Starck has made an unusual contribution to modern-day bathroom culture. The originality of the design lies in getting back to essentials, doing away with all that is superfluous, and the return to simple forms that have always been associated with water: the bucket, hand pump and washing bowl. With his intuition for the style of things to come and the return to traditional forms, Philippe Starck has given the bathroom a completely new lease of life. The result is an unusual bathroom which creates a unique ambience, with practical technical details for improved hygienic comfort. However, this is only a side effect, not the main concern. Philippe Starck's hallmark is the philosophy of omission, which leads to a design that appears both familiar and yet new.

Design Awards 2002: iF Design Award for Happy D., Industrie Forum Design (Germany) / red dot for washbasin Philippe Starck and wash basin Vero, Design Zentrum Nordrhein Westfalen (Germany)

Design Awards 2001: Bundespreis Produktdesign for Philippe Starck Edition 1, Rat für Formgebung (Germany)

Design Awards 2000: Good Design Award for Happy D., The Chicago Athenaeum: Museum of Architecture and Design (USA) / Red Dot for High Design Quality for wash basin Dreamscape, Design Zentrum Nordrhein Westfalen (Germany)

Design Awards 1999: Red Dot for the Highest Design Quality for a wash basin by Philippe Starck, Design Zentrum Nordrhein Westfalen (Germany) / Red Dot for High Design Quality for washbasin from the Starck Edition 2, Design Zentrum Nordrhein Westfalen (Germany)

Design Awards 1998: for the Philippe Starck Edition 1, Good Design Award, Museum of Architecture and Design Chicago (USA) / iF Design Award, Industrie Forum Design (Germany) / Red Dot for High Design Quality, Design Zentrum Nordrhein Westfalen (Germany)

Philippe Starck Edition 2: Uncomplicated design characterises the sanitary products of Starck Edition 2. The flowing shapes echo the motions of water, reminding one of water rings and whirlpools. With his own characteristic ease, Starck brings the spirit of form to life with reduction and simplicity. The complete range encompasses a wealth of variations, and opens up a new dimension for an individual bather's wishes – including the wish for good design expressing the joy and quality of life, even in the smaller bathroom or on a tight budget.

Happy D.: Outstanding new products bring with them a pleasing kind of recognition factor. This is almost always due to styling which ensures that the original is perceived as the design model for things to come. "Less is more" – achieved by concentrating on the essentials and giving them new form and expression. Dieter and Michael Sieger have rediscovered the original concept: a true archetype. The bathroom with universal appeal, one that is generally and internationally recognisable, imparts a true feeling of rediscovering something which has been lost. The geometric shape makes the products unmistakable archetypes of bathroom design. Viewed from the top, all the products in the range take on the shape of a "D".

Christian Klingspor,
Senior Vice President
of Design

Sweden

AB Electrolux

S:t Göransgatan 143
Stockholm
Tel. +46 8 738 6000
Fax +46 8 738 4478
www.electrolux.com

Electrolux

The Electrolux Corporate Design Team currently employs 130 design professionals and is active in 13 locations around the world. The award winning team provides strategic and practical design support for the Electrolux Group, the world's largest manufacturer of household appliances. More than 55 million Electrolux Group products are sold each year in more than 150 countries around the world.

Electrolux has a longstanding tradition of effective design management evidenced by its early use of designers such as Raymond Loewy and later Sixten Sason. Electrolux grew to its current size through a series of key acquisitions including the WCI Group in North America, Zanussi, Thorn EMI and AEG in Europe, Prosdòcimo in Brazil and more recently Email in Australia. The acquisitions brought with them a rich tapestry of cultural diversity and heritage but also new design teams with their own values and beliefs, for instance AEG was one of the first companies to take a integral approach to design management with

Peter Behrens, later a founder member of the Bauhaus movement. For Electrolux, the early establishment of an internal group design management in 1964, run by Hugo Lindström, contributed to the global success. He is one of the pioneers of industrial design in Sweden. Since 1985, the teams have been managed as a corporate design group headed by Christian Klingspor, Senior Vice President of Design.

The design management team headed by C. Klingspor has structured the organisation into 6 design centres located in North America: Anderson, USA, Rick Weiss, General Manager / Bloomington, IL, USA, headed by Randal Sandlin, Design Director / South America: Curitiba, Brazil, headed by Julio Bertola, Design Director / Australia: Sydney, headed by Lars Erikson, Design Director / China Changsha, headed from Stockholm by Andrew Cameron, Design Director / Europe: Porcia, Italy, headed by Sean Carney, Design Director / Stockholm, Sweden (Floor care products), headed by Per Börjesson, Design Director / (Outdoor products) headed by Towe Ressman, Design Director.
The team is aided in its activities by Roberto Pezzetta who as Vice President Design provides creative design direction.

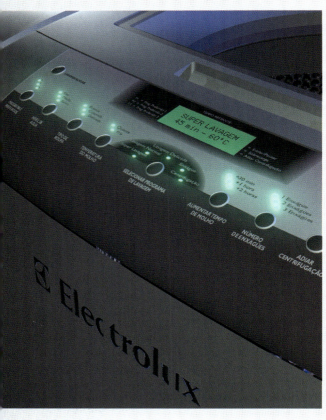

Top loader washing machine from Brazil

The design centres provide the main strategic design support for the Electrolux Group and are complemented by a network of smaller design studios in key locations througout the world. Design management responsibility is divided into the key business areas of household products, such as refrigerators, washing machines, ovens, vacuum cleaners and also outdoor products such as garden and forest equipment (lawnmowers and chainsaws).

Electrolux Corporate Design has contributed to the high levels of success the group has achieved in profitable business growth. It has also been recognised for a high level of design integrity winning many international design competitions including the following: iF Design Award, Industrie Forum Design (Germany) / Compasso d'oro (Italy) / Janus de l'Industrie, Institut Français du Design (France) / I. D. Magazine Award (USA) / Good Design Award, Museum of Architecture and Design Chicago (USA) / Goed Industrieel Ontweerp Award (Netherlands) / Utmaerkt Svensk Form (Sweden) / Bio Ljubljana (Slovenia) / red dot award: product design, Design Zentrum Nordrhein Westfalen (Germany).

In a process of global collaboration between the design centres emerging markets are identified at an early stage and new technologies evaluated. The teams are active in stimulating new markets by means of exploratory studies on future products. Concept studies have been created by generating future scenarios which explore the socioeconomic and demographic developments alongside technological advances. The concepts create road maps for potential future markets. The future for the Electrolux Corporate Design Team will be in acting as a stimulus creating global and local products that create and fulfil consumer demands in current and future markets. The team is set to continue its pursuit of excellence in all processes in order to provide the Electrolux Group companies with innovative and marketable products.

R 310 refrigerator from Brazil

Westinghouse Virtuoso refrigerator from Australia

Long before the technical concept of ergonomy became established in the world of product design, Fiskars produced garden utensils which convinced by their light weight, simple handling and lifetime guarantee. The Finnish shears, distinguished by their bright orange-red handles, are ideal for all who work in a garden and soon became established as classic gardening tools. It is possible to work with the geared hedge shears for a long time without fatigue. This tool weighs only 730 grams. The blades are made of hardened stainless steel. The oval lever arms are made of glass fibre reinforced polyamide. The anti-adhesion coated cutting surface reduces friction. Buffers reduce stress on the joints. The lever transmission does not stress the arm muscles more than necessary, even when cutting with the tips of the shears. Even persons who only occasionally work in the garden appreciate the peace and relaxation of working in the open air. The geared hedge shear from Fiskars makes gardening a pleasure without any negative side effects.

Fiskars

Finland

Fiskars Consumer Oy Ab

10330 Billnäs, Finland
Tel. +358-19 / 277-721
Fax +358-19 / 230 986
www.fiskars.com

More than 350 years ago, Fiskars was founded by the river with the same name in the south of Finland. Already in the 1820's the fine forging workshop produced iron forgings like tableware, scissors and kitchen knives. Fiskars' international breakthrough came in 1967 with the orange-handled Classic scissors, later to become world-famous and still today to be recognised as a symbol of high-quality Fiskars products. Since 1649 Fiskars has evolved into an internationally successful and diverse company with subsidiaries all over the world. The tools are widely used for cooking, gardening, crafting, hunting, fishing and camping both by occasional and frequent users.

Innovation is the key to Fiskars' success in all product categories. Continuous product development and extensive research in areas such as consumer ergonomics and material recycling has resulted in numerous design awards both in Europe and the United States. Excellent materials guarantee the durability of Fiskars products and the ergonomic design ensures that the tools are easy and comfortable to use.

Unique inventions have been made in human history - some of them can be reinvented and many still remain to be discovered. Extensive studies and careful testing combined with "nature's planned coincidence" will be the basis for Fiskars product development also in the future.

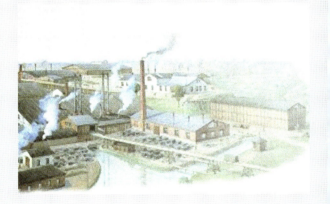

Mexico

**GRUPO D.I.,
S. DE R.L. DE C.V.**

Altavista 119
Colonia San Angel Inn
01060 México D. F.
Tel. +52 55 616-07 70
Fax +52 55 550-64 97
info@grupodi.com
www.grupodi.com

Grupo Di

In 1970, grupo di started operations with a qualified team of office space planners, on Altavista Street in San Angel Inn, in the southwest of Mexico City. The changes of the trade agreements in Mexico during the late 1980s allowed grupo di to establish strategic business relationships with a group of important Italian manufacturers to build a factory in Mexico. This facility has enabled them to support their fast delivery programme since 1993, offering customers a wide variety of high quality options at short notice.

A working environment based on quality and service is the bond between 120 employees, three showrooms and a factory producing furniture to international quality standards. grupo di is a company that blends two ingredients: youth and experience. This formula has proved over the years to be successful and has yielded a team of professional office space planners. Customers feel reassured by the commitment of a second generation family business whose main objective is customer service.

grupo di is aware of the importance of having an internationally recognised quality assurance system and therefore since November 2000 the firm's quality system has been certified to the ISO 9001 Standard (ANSI / ASQC Q9001-1994). This makes grupo di one of the first Latin American office furniture manufacturers to obtain such certification, and the first one in Mexico. grupo di offers solutions for the Mexican market based on avant-garde concepts with the adequate balance between functionality and image. This combination results in efficient and productive workspaces. The team of 15 industrial designers continues to research and develop new elements to complement grupo di's office furniture system.

podio is grupo di's periodic publication, created to satisfy the need for communication on office interior space planning in Mexico. podio deals with things that constitute interior space planning; from the space to the objects that give shape to it. The magazine is divided into sections that include the most important subjects for office and contract interiors: new spaces, products, techniques and opinions that set new standards.

Maria Aurora Campos
de Diaz and
Lorenzo Diaz Campos

Maria Aurora Campos de Diaz was the first industrial designer to graduate from Universidad Iberoamericana in Mexico City in 1962. In 1964 she studied at the University of Southern California (USC) in the department of industrial design. She received a scholarship awarded by the Italian government for the Politecnico di Milano in 1964. She studied in the Hochschule für Gestaltung (HfG) Ulm from 1967 to 1968 with a scholarship awarded by the German government (DAAD) and founded grupo di in 1970. She was a founding member of the Asociación de Diseñadores Mexicanos (DIMAC) in 1971 and set up podio magazine in 1991. She has been an active advocate of Mexican and European design in Mexico collaborating in several magazines and giving lectures at different design congresses. She was included in the book "Frauen im Design 1', published for the touring exhibition for the Design Center Stuttgart in October of 1989.

Lorenzo Diaz Campos was born in Mexico City in 1969. He received the award Premio Nacional de la Juventud 1985 in the creative and invention category from the hands of the President of Mexico. He gained his international baccalaureate (IB) at the United World College of the Adriatic with a scholarship awarded by the Italian Foreign Ministry. In 1989 he abandoned undergraduate school and his industrial design studies to join the family business at the age of 20.

Euro Sistema: In 1999 grupo di developed euro sistema, launching it in June 2000 and receiving an excellent response. This system results from the interplay between today's main parameters: technology and functionality. euro sistema blends into the work environment with practical solutions that combine the adaptability to technological systems with highly resistant materials. This combination of interesting forms – in a wide variety of finishes – satisfies the needs of any office environment in Mexico.
The system is divided into four main lines: euro scrivanie, euro pannelli, euro contenitori and euro reunión. Systems like euro sistema are not the result of an accident. The experience and constant research of grupo di's design team are reflected in euro sistema, a complete system to meet every office space need without sacrificing productivity and comfort. The ergonomic lines and wise selection of materials make euro sistema the highlight that harmonises with any office environment. Technology, design, quality and functionality for the office space in one system. A coordinated range comprising free-standing desks, workstations, storage and filing units, and meeting tables.

Hungary

Herend Porcelain Manufactory Ltd.

Kossuth Layos St. 140
8440 Herend
Tel. +36-88 / 523-100
Fax +36-88 / 261-518
info@herend.com
www.herend.com

Herend Porcelain

Since its inception in 1826, Herend has been producing one of the world's most distinctive porcelains. The signature of Herend is named after the picturesque Hungarian village where it is made. The manufactory has long been admired for its handcrafted, hand-painted porcelain works of art. Herend found its true niche in the mid-19th century, at a time when the Hungarian market was flooded with low-cost pottery. Instead, it made its mark with refined, classic dinnerware comparable to the most superior hard-paste porcelain products of the time. So began an enduring reputation as the supplier of choice for exquisite dinnerware, found worldwide in the homes of royalty, celebrities and connoisseurs of life's finest things.

Building on its dinnerware success, Herend extended its artistic offerings in the 1860s, introducing meticulously crafted figurines. The animal kingdom of Herend is peopled with endearing creatures meek and bold, large and small, loveable and fearsome. There they share space with an eclectic community of vibrant folk figurines depicting the lifestyles of old. In a modern world, Herend continues to rely on the formula that has earned it its reputation over 175 years: a hard-paste porcelain body, unique craftsmanship, exceptional attention to detail and intricate artistry.

The company was privatised in 1993 under an employee share-ownership scheme, with a minority stake still held by the Hungarian state. The Manufactory has become a privately owned joint-stock company employing some 1600 persons, running a century-old trade school of its own. The Manufactory is noted for its achievements in the fields of quality and environmental management, for which it has received a number of Hungarian and foreign awards. It has also been awarded the distinction of being part of the Hungarian Heritage. The studio and workshops of the Manufactory provide opportunities for Hungarian and foreign ceramic artists to experiment and create outstanding works of art in porcelain.

Service by Pálma Babos: Pálma Babos graduated from the ceramics department of the Hungarian College of Applied Arts in 1985, after studying under Imre Schrammel. Like her master, she has been working at Herend since 1996. Her patterns and services mark an effective and sensitive renewal of the art of Herend Porcelain. One of the finest of all is the service in Babos pattern. The charming, supple vessels have handles inspired by the pose of a bird turning backwards to preen its feathers. The swirling motifs painted in blue and gold augment the richly gilded, pierced bases and the handles and spouts.

Cups by Miklós Melocco Miklós Melocco graduated in sculpture from the Hungarian College of Fine Art in 1961. He has made countless statues and small sculptures in a career stretching over four decades, receiving the prestigious Kossuth Prize in 1988. Melocco has been doing work for the Herend Porcelain Manufactory since the 1990s. The best known of his creations for Herend, a tea service, is a splendid blend of local tradition and the sculptor's own style. The service is covered with a traditional Herend pattern of scales, but the handles and finials are shaped as hands that allude to the human purpose of tea and coffee drinking.

Soup tureen in ROEV pattern by Imre Schrammel As a ceramicist, Imre Schrammel does not confine himself to large-scale sculptures. He also makes attractive smaller sculptures and vessels that set out to combine his figures with the Herend Porcelain Manufactory's traditional patterns and shapes. There is evidence of this endeavour in his soup tureen in Rothschild décor augmented with a green scale pattern. The cover, adorned with birds and butterflies, also shows Carnival clowns in garments decorated with the well-known Rothschild motifs. The composition adds an extra dimension to a splendid and cheerful pattern.

Orchestra by László Fekete László Fekete, a member of the younger generation of Herend artists, has been working at Herend for four years. His first work was to design twelve tiny figures in a naïve, archaic style, signifying the signs of the Zodiac. The ensemble seen here came next. In these figures shaped in a humorous fashion, the artist has expressed the characters of the musicians through aptly expressed movements and symbols. Here he has used a special technique to produce these little pieces of pierced porcelain.

USA

IBM Corporation

Route 100, CSB – CB 125
Somers, New York 10589
Tel. +1 914 766-05 15
Fax +1 914 766-90 14
ldgreen@us.ibm.com
www.ibm.com

IBM

IBM Corporate Design and the rebuilding of the IBM Brand. A statement by Lee Green, IBM Director of Corporate Identity and Design

Thomas Watson Jr. once said, "Great design will not sell an inferior product, but it will enable it to achieve its maximum potential." Conversely, I believe a bad design may achieve some success because of excellent marketing, or discount pricing, but its success almost always fails to endure, and it seldom achieves greatness. I think we see products today that major on the superficial, and minor on "customer value". At IBM, our focus remains on creating enduring value: the combination of elegant design and intelligent, new user experience.

The role of design at IBM has gone through several significant transitions since the mid-1950s when design consultants Eliot Noyes, Paul Rand and Charles Eames influenced virtually every design decision made in the company. By the late 1980s, design and branding decisions had been largely delegated to over a dozen different operating units across IBM. The result was an erosion in both design quality and image. The IBM design function had also lost much of its influence and credibility. When Lou Gerstner arrived at IBM we presented a visual audit to him that demonstrated how IBM was being "collectively" viewed by our customers. This audit included a representation of how we were presenting IBM in the marketplace, via our logos, advertising, naming, product design, exhibits, publications, etc. The key here is the collective, aggregate level view. What we found was that because design decisions were being made transactionally, or execution by execution, the result was a fractured presentation of the IBM brand. Customers told us that this fractured visual presentation also sent the signal that IBM was not operating cohesively – that one IBM group did not work with the other IBM group.

This does not mean that all the design that was being produced in the late 1980s was bad. On the contrary, some was excellent. But design was not operating as an effective, strategic, integrated discipline across the business. Mr. Gerstner recognised this immediately, and recognised that the same operational problems existed across IBM.

Lee Green is the Director of Corporate Identity and Design for IBM Corporation. He has been in this position since 1993, when Lou Gerstner became CEO of IBM. He has responsibility for IBM's worldwide product industrial design, identity programmes, graphics, packaging and Internet design. Mr. Green has played a pivotal role in recent Branding and Design initiatives including the launch of IBM's new e-business identity programme and the redesign of IBM's desktop, mobile, and server products. He also leads the corporation's efforts in the area of "advanced concept design".

In his 23-year career with IBM he has held numerous design and communications management positions. Mr. Green has an undergraduate degree in design from Temple University and a master's degree in Communications Design from Rochester Institute of Technology. He has published numerous articles and case studies on a variety of design and identity topics, and has taught design courses and lectured on design at Stanford University, Harvard, MIT and RIT. He currently serves on the Board of Directors for the Design Management Institute and as an advisor to the University of Westminster MBA programme.

As a result, there was a strategic shift in philosophy that emphasised the importance of rebuilding a strong, integrated, single IBM brand and leveraging IBM's collective strengths. Design has played a significant role in that revitalisation effort, with a focus on all of IBM's visual expressions. The corporate design function has once again become pro-active, and influential in setting design strategy, and stimulating business strategy. This has been aided by Mr. Gerstner's focus on revitalising the IBM brand. Progress in reestablishing design credibility has also occurred because the corporate design function now performs less of an "approval" role, and more of a "value-adding" and strategic role. This has led to a renewed focus on IBM's design principles and an elevated mission for IBM designers, who serve as customer advocates. Design in IBM now functions as a strategic component of our marketing initiatives. No longer are designers engaged at the end of the development process. Today, IBM designers play an active role in stimulating decisions regarding which products or identity initiatives will be pursued next. One current identity design example is "e-business". By creating the e -business term and IBM's red-e logo, IBM was able to create a new market category, and to emerge as the leader in providing integrated e-business hardware, software and services. This strategic identity initiative allowed us to signal our focus and our positioning, internally and externally, and helped make IBM synonymous with e-business. Design has played a vital role in leading both the creation of the e-business identity for IBM, and in charting a course for use of this identity that has built recognition, equity and unique association with IBM.

IBM's first and most important design principle emphasises the need to begin any design initiative by understanding both customer needs and customer aspirations. This process involves the synthesis of the user context and technology context. It also requires a clear articulation of explicit customer scenarios, before any design project is initiated. This approach is applied to all IBM design.
For example, when we redesigned our PC and Server products we conducted ethnographic, observational research to better understand how people interacted with our products, and how they worked. We examined our manufacturing, development, and distribution processes. And we conducted multiple research sessions with customers and IBM partners to gain knowledge that would allow us to iterate and modify the designs. The application of this principle also has significant influence on all of our strategic design activity. Done right, it can provide insights that lead to unique differentiation, and breakthrough products which create new market opportunities.

The second principle deals with our design image, or visual language. Here the focus remains on pure geometry, simplicity and emotional appeal. Sometimes this manifests itself in "whimsical" form. Often the result is a design impression that signals strength, reliability and coherence. Regardless of style or personality, IBM's design decisions are always intended to reflect authenticity, via purposeful form. This contrasts with much of the superficial design seen on the market today. Products that may capture attention but provide little enduring value.
Customers tell us that our eServers look and function like sophisticated business machines. That they are easier to set up, to repair, to upgrade and to maintain than any of our competitors' servers. They perceive that design and usability are a high priority for IBM. I believe the "sweet spot" in market success is where it has always been. Make it easier for a customer to do something that was difficult before. Simplify their lives, eliminate complexity, make them feel good about using your product. These attributes distinguish the breakthroughs from everything else. They also build loyalty, and allow for differentiation, enabling competition on more than price alone.

The last principle has to do with "vision". Thinking in big shifts. Filtering all the knowledge about how people want to work, along with all that is possible, given emerging technologies. And creating visions of the future. The automobile industry refers to this as "concept car" design, or advanced design. It is this process and applied principle that has led to design solutions like IBM's Wearable Computer, or concepts like the e-newspaper that imagine a new world of function specific e-business enabled devices. The e-newspaper prototype depicts the future possibilities of electronic news retrieval, from multiple publications, all delivered by a single news aggregator. The concept depicts a flexible display, rather than a glass TFT display, enabled by a new generation of organic technology from IBM. Other technologies, like embedded voice, high-density microdrive storage, Blue Tooth wireless communications and miniaturised optical viewers, all contribute to future design concepts that will facilitate a new world of convenience and natural computing. We believe that our customers expect to work with a technology company that helps them visualise the implementation of these emerging technologies in ways that they, have not considered.

Collectively, the rigorous focus on these principles has helped IBM regain the design leadership position it held decades ago. This success has also been made possible by several additional factors. Firstly, a restructuring of IBM's design organisation, with designers reporting to marketing so that decisions can be evaluated in a customer context. Secondly, our internal designer and external consultant skills. Newly assigned IBM design management, "best-of-breed" internal IBM design talent, and the guidance and mentorship of our Corporate Consultant, Richard Sapper. In today's IBM environment, designers have renewed credibility, and as a result are often in a position to stimulate the next generation of offerings from IBM. This has proven to be good for IBM's customers, and good for IBM.

iittala

Finland

iittala

Designor Oy Ab
P.O. Box
FIN-00561 Helsinki
Tel. +358 204 39-11
Fax +358 204 39-57 42
iittala.info@designor.com
www.iittala.fi

The iittala glass factory was established in 1881, and the iittala brand was born in 1956 when Timo Sarpaneva designed the red "i" for his new collection of modern utility glass. The collection was awarded the Grand Prix at the Milan Triennale. The "i" soon became the symbol of all of iittala's products. In the 1950s, the concept of "Finnish Design" was established worldwide. iittala had great success in various international exhibitions, for instance in the Triennale of Milan. The products, like Tapio Wirkkala's Chantarelle and Timo Sarpaneva's Orchid grew to be classics both in Finland and abroad. At the end of the 1980s, the ownership of the iittala glassworks changed. Iittala and Nuutajärvi glass factories were merged, and in 1990 HackmanGroup bought Iittala-Nuutajärvi. Today, Hackman Group's glass, porcelain and stainless steel factories have been combined into a single unit called Designor Oy Ab. Besides iittala there are three other Scandinavian brands, Arabia, Hackman and Rörstrand, in the same company.

As a result of this development, the range of iittala products has grown to cover all elements of dining and cooking. Dinnerware, cutlery and cookware are now a part of the iittala assortment. Fine examples of iittala's products include the Aalto vase (Alvar Aalto, 1936), Teema dinnerware (Kaj Franck, 1981), tools® Dahlström 98 cookware (Björn Dahlström, 1998), tools® Citterio 98 cutlery (Antonio Citterio, 1998), Grcic glasses (Konstantin Grcic 1999) and Origo between the meals concept (Alfredo Häberli, 1999) among others.

There have been numerous awards given to iittala's design, beginning with the international shows in Milan in the 1950s. Here are just a few examples of the latest international awards. The Design Plus Award has been given to iittala's products several times at the international Ambiente Fair in Frankfurt, Germany. Design Plus is awarded by Messe Frankfurt GmbH.

Origo, 1999

tools® Dahlström 98, 1998

Grcic, 1999

In 2002 it went to the Essence decanter (Alfredo Häberli), in 2001 to the tools® Citterio Collective tools cutlery range (Antonio Citterio) and in 2000 to the tools® Lovegrove 99 water kettle (Ross Lovegrove) and the Grcic glasses (Konstantin Grcic).

The iF Product Design Award for the year 2002 went to tools® Lovegrove 2000 cookware (Ross Lovegrove), ProfPan cookware (Björn Dahlström) and the Origo between the meals concept (Alfredo Häberli).

Previously, the iF Product Design Award was given to tools® Citterio 2000 (Antonio Citterio) and tools® Citterio Collective tools (Antonio Citterio) in the year 2001 and to tools® Lovegrove 99 (Ross Lovegrove) in 2000.

The Good Design Award by the Chicago Athenaeum, USA, was given to tools® Piano 98 (Renzo Piano Workshop), tools® Citterio 98 (Antonio Citterio), tools® Citterio 2000 (Antonio Citterio), tools® Citterio Collective tools (Antonio Citterio) and tools® Lovegrove 2000 (Ross Lovegrove) in 2000. Yet each piece of iittala assortment strongly reflects the personal creativity of its designer. iittala's history demonstrates that success depends on having the courage to make new kinds of objects.

iittala   Hall of Fame   73

Norway

Intra AS

Storsand
N-7563 Malvik
Tel. +47 739 80-100
Fax +47 739 80-150
intra@intra-group.com
www.intra-group.com

Intra

Intra was established in Trondheim, Norway, in 1947 and is a family owned and family run company. In addition to the headquarters in Trondheim, the business has manufacturing plants in Denmark, Sweden, Germany and a sales company in Poland. Intra is the leading manufacturer of kitchen sinks in the Nordic area and the company is well known for its elegant and functional designs.

The material used is stainless steel, a material with unique qualities, particularly in environments where there are strict demands with regard to hygiene and durability, such as bathrooms, toilets and kitchens in both private homes and public facilities. There is a requirement for sinks that harmonise with and enhance modern kitchen and bathroom designs. New designs and materials are gaining a foothold and the trend is towards hygienic stainless steel in kitchens, bathrooms and public sanitary facilities. Intra's commitment to design has resulted in functional products and aesthetically pleasing forms. "We have developed an advanced technology that enables us to stamp out stainless steel in almost any shape a designer may wish to achieve." Intra and designer Odd Thorsen received awards for good design as far back as 1985. The company's goal has always been to maintain traditions and functional properties, but at the same time to allow the products to take on their own identity. Intra was proclaimed Design Company of the Year in Norway in 1987.

Eurora: In 1997 Eurora received the Award for Good Design. The design has been further developed and sinks are now available for all types of kitchen – regardless of size and fittings. The combination of a traditional rectangular pattern and a modern organic shape has resulted in a unique design.

Intra Millinox™ is a new range of sanitary equipment in stainless steel. This is a complete concept for public sanitary facilities and represents the cutting edge in Norwegian design. This might be the reason why Intra Millinox™ sanitary equipment was chosen for the Norwegian pavilion at the World Exhibition in Hanover – Expo 2000. Millinox™ provides countless opportunities for new and innovative solutions – the concept encompasses everything from the simplest products to integrated touch-free units. Intra Millinox received the Award for Good Design in 2001 and has achieved a high degree of recognition on the market.

Spain

Irizar S. Coop

Zumarraga Bidea, 8.
20216 Ormaiztegi
Gipuzkoa
Tel. +34 943 80 91 00
Fax +34 943 88 91 01
irizar@irizar.com
www.irizar.com

Irizar

Irizar's origins as a horse-drawn carriage maker date from the year 1889, when traditional craft and metalworking skills were used to make single bespoke vehicles. These techniques have gradually evolved into the state-of-the-art techniques and processes it uses today, while the care, customised approach and attention to detail are still a feature of its work on each one of the coaches it builds. Irizar manufactures luxury coaches which it markets in 65 countries, as a result of agreements with distributors worldwide, and its international expansion which began in 1995. Based at Ormaiztegi (Spain), the Irizar Group has subsidiaries in Brazil, Mexico and Morrocco. 2400 people make up the Irizar Group.

Individualistic exterior and interior designs have become an Irizar trademark. Its coaches have won awards throughout Europe for their product quality and innovation, examples of which are: Coach of the Year Awards in Brighton, (United Kingdom, 1994 and 1997) and Madrid (Spain, 1994) / Prince Philip of Asturias Award for Business Excellence in Industrial Design, Ministry of Trade and Industry (Spain, 1995) / Coach chosen to transport the teams taking part in the Football World Cup (France, 1998) / Coach selected for the exhibition "100 Years of Industrial Design in Spain" in the Queen Sofía Museum, Ministries of Education and Culture / Industry and Energy, (Spain,1998).

Irizar's management structure is different from that of other companies, and its driving force lies in its approach, its "project based on people". This is what has made Irizar one of the most prosperous companies in Spain, undisputed leader in its sector in Spain and second in Europe.

Proof of the company's great success can be found in the number of Spanish and international recognitions received for its management and achievements. Irizar was, for example, the first European company in its sector to achieve the ISO 9001 (1994) and ISO 14001 certifications (1998). After being the first company to win the top awards for Business Management Excellence in both Spain (1996) and in the Basque Country (1999), it went on to achieve the European Quality Prize (EFQM-European Foundation for Quality Management, Istanbul, 2000).

The Irizar PB coach is robust, aerodynamic and safe. It was designed to meet customer needs for safety, comfort, reliability and cost-effectiveness.

This coach fully complies with existing and future European regulations. Its stability and improved rigidity, rollover and head-on impact resistance, torsional strength, and the reduction of glass surface in the vehicle guarantee safety. As for comfort, the boarding points are wider, the driver and passenger areas are extremely spacious. The automatic air conditioning system creates two different temperature levels for the driver and passengers.

With the excellent insulation, aerodynamic and ergonomic designs create a quiet and cosy environment inside the vehicle. The latest materials, technologies and modular designs provide the coach with maximum reliability. This new coach offers real cost-effectiveness, with exceedingly low fuel consumption, economical and interchangeable spares.

Timothy Jacob Jensen and Jacob Jensen

Denmark

JACOB JENSEN DESIGN

Hejlskovvej 104
7840 Højslev
Tel. +45 97 53 86 00
Fax +45 97 53 85 28
hq@jacobjensen.com
www.jacobjensen.com

JACOB JENSEN DESIGN

In 1958, Jacob Jensen established the studio Jacob Jensen Design in Copenhagen, Denmark. He was originally trained as a furniture designer, graduating from the School of Applied Art in 1952. Among his teachers were some of the most distinguished Danish craftsmen, designers and architects: Kaare Klindt, Jørn Utzon and Hans J. Wegner.

Jacob Jensen has always had a sense of humour and curiosity, characteristics which have led him to ask questions. Questions like: what would happen if you turned this upside down? How would it look, how would it function? Can it be smaller, smoother, lighter, take up less space? Today, half a century later, we know that Jacob Jensen's questions brought new answers, new solutions to the world of industrial design.

One of the earliest of these solutions is the Margrethe bowl, a simple kitchen mixing bowl which is still being produced – because it works, and because it embodies a quiet beauty. Jacob Jensen received particular recognition for the extensive line of audio products he created for Bang & Olufsen, for whom he worked from 1964 to 1991. With a language of form which was innovative and recognised on a global scale, he became one of the few industrial designers in the world to be chosen by the Museum of Modern Art in New York for a solo exhibition. The 1978 exhibition was entitled "Bang & Olufsen – Design for sound by Jacob Jensen" and included 28 audio products.

Possessing the same skills and talent as Jacob, his son Timothy Jacob Jensen was apprenticed to his father in 1978 and took over Jacob Jensen Design in 1989. Under his leadership the studio has been interpreting the Scandinavian values and tradition in depth and is today recognised as one of the leading design consultancies in the world. Its numerous creations include the design of a total programme of kitchen appliances from 1991 to 1998 for the German company Gaggenau. These products have created a conceptual and visual foundation for Gaggenau; products which have been acclaimed and received awards for high quality design.

As Jacob Jensen has often pointed out, when you hold a stone axe in your hand you know what the person who made it 6000 years ago was thinking: What do I need, how can I make it? Nothing more, nothing less. Today the studio is still committed to the basic "stone axe" principle of simple, straight-forward communication and usability, incorporating the designer's silent signature.

To quote Timothy: "One of the eternal laws of our planet is action - reaction; in nature and in culture. A creation demands a reaction. The success of a creation is dependent upon commitment, idea, communication and the evolutionary process until perfection is reached. Being aware of these components one can achieve results which reduce vulnerability and strengthen recognition and survival. It is in fact very simple."

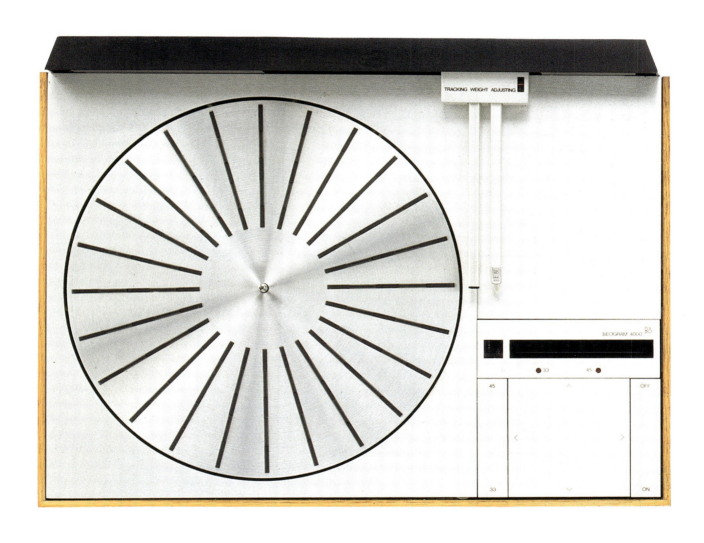

Beogram 4000
Bang & Olufsen, 1972

Beomaster 1900
Bang & Olufsen, 1976

Beocenter 9000
Bang & Olufsen, 1987

JACOB JENSEN Timer clock
Bell Xpress and S. Weisz, 2002

EB 900 Built-in oven Gaggenau, 1993

Margrethe Bowl Rosti – Design by Jacob Jensen for Bernadotte & Bjørn, 1955

JACOB JENSEN Classic watch series
model no.510 - 520, Max René, 1986

Germany

Kärcher

Alfred Kärcher GmbH & Co.

Alfred Kärcher Straße 28-40
71364 Winnenden
Tel. +49 7195 14-0
Fax +49 7195 14-22 12
info@kaercher.com
www.kaercher.com

"For a cleaner world" is the motto of Alfred Kärcher GmbH &Co. in Winnenden near Stuttgart. The family company, which was founded in 1935, develops, produces and distributes cleaning technology and equipment for many fields of application. Kärcher products such as pressure washers, vacuum cleaners, steam cleaners, sweepers and scrubber-driers, cleaning agents, vehicle washes and wastewater treatment units are becoming increasingly popular with professional and industrial users as well as municipal authorities and private households. Since it decided to concentrate on cleaning technology in 1974, the company has become a specialist in this field, operating on a global basis. With its continually expanding sales and marketing structure which at present comprises 34 companies at home and abroad and 36,000 service points in more than 130 countries, Kärcher's turnover has grown considerably over the last 3 decades. Today, Kärcher has a staff of more than 5,500 worldwide. Innovation is Kärcher's single most important growth factor. Some 75 % of all its products are only four years old or younger. This is evidence of the high level of creativity on the part of the 280 engineers and technicians who work in the company's design centres using leading edge know-how and technology.

When Kärcher brought out the world's first portable pressure washer, for example, it created a completely new market. For this achievement, Kärcher was awarded the German Marketing Prize in 1997. Another factor which guarantees Kärcher's continued successful growth is the high standard of precision and quality of its products, as evidenced by the DIN EN ISO 9001 certification the company has received.

Environmental protection is one more area where Kärcher has become an industry pacesetter. In 1996, it was one of the first companies in the cleaning equipment industry to receive the international DIN EN ISO 14001 certification for its environmental management system. Kärcher's track record in the field of product design is also a successful one. Time and again the company has received international prizes such as the "red dot" or the "iF product design" awards. Kärcher products are not, however, designed only for good looks. At Kärcher, design is seen as a combination of attractive styling, functionality and ergonomics and has long been an integral part of the development process. Kärcher will continue to concentrate on cleaning technology in the future. And innovation will still be the decisive growth factor, so that the Kärcher brand will remain what it is today: a synonym for cleanliness.

K 670 MS plus: Pressure Washer

Korea

LG Electronics

LG Electronics

Digital Design Center
LG Kangnam Tower 679
Yoksam-dong, Kangnam-gu,
135-080, Seoul
Tel. +82 2 20 05-31 10
Fax +82 2 20 05-31 15
www.lge.com

The LG Electronics company is now in its 44th year of existence. When it started out in 1958, there were almost no industry facilities available nationwide. During these 44 years, people at LG Electronics have constantly faced uphill challenges, and their achievements have not only placed LG at the leading edge but also contributed to raising the standards of the Korean electronic industry. Beginning with the first domestically produced radio soon after the company's establishment, LG Electronics has achieved a reputation for being the first on the market. TV sets, refrigerators, air-conditioners, telephones, and many more "firsts" in home appliances have since followed, all setting new standards in the domestic electronics sector. At the end of 1990s the company grew to be unrivalled in the field of displays, including high-end digital TVs, PDPs and mobile devices for CDMA. Producing technological breakthroughs, LG systematically pursued its goal of becoming a worldwide digital leader.

At LG Electronics, design is seen as an integral component of the long-term strategy: "By investing in design, we invest in our future. In our new vision for the millennium we declare our commitment to make design one of our core competencies, an essential step in our drive to be counted among the world's foremost electronics and IT companies." The LG Electronics Digital Design Center was established in 1983, followed in the early 1990s by satellite studios in Europe, North America and elsewhere in Asia, and the new design centre was established in Milan, Italy, in March 2002.

Since 1999, Digital LG, the vision for the new millennium of LG, has shown that LG regards design as a strategic tool at corporate management level. Design is deployed as an efficient tool for enhancing the products' competitiveness and creating added value for the products in an era of technology generalisation. As a tribute to the strategic significance of design in LG, the LG Digital Design Center was moved to the new Kangnam Tower in a splendid business and culture district, providing a new interior environment to enhance the designers' creativity. The company has no doubt that such a change on such a meaningful occasion – the beginning of new millennium – will provide the designers with better fundamentals for creative design excellence. To this end, following the inauguration of "Digital LG" in 1999, they rededicated themselves to their vision in early 2002 under the motto of "First-Class LG".

Multinet X Desktop PC: The luxurious appearance of the housing composed of ABS material is emphasised by its round style. The large half mirror on the front radiates a light in a calm blue tone whenever there is a movement caught on the screen. The whole appearance of the product is simple since the CD-ROM part is covered with different materials. It takes up 30 percent less space than other compact PCs and reduces overheating and noise to 27.32 DB.

G-510 Mobile Phone: A flat, wafer-thin 18mm enhances usability. Moreover, it is designed to be opened with one hand. Since this product has a slim and compact shape with light weight (70g), and an 8-lined wide display, checking information becomes easier. The side structure lets you open it with one hand. The mobile also features a WAP browser.

MW-30LZ10 with 30" wide LCD TV offers a wide range interface and multi-compatible applications: VGA-SXGA PC signals input.

DIOS Internet Refrigerator: The built-in 15.1" LCD screen on this high-end digital refrigerator features audio and video functions like TV and other display screens. It accesses image and text message transmissions that facilitate grocery orders, recipe searching and downloading, home shopping, e-mails, and interconnection and control of other home appliances via the Internet and a home server.

V-C 750 Vacuum Cleaner Cyking: A cylinder-type bagless vacuum cleaner that uses the cyclone system. CYKING provides the world's strongest suction power in a cyclone system vacuum cleaner. It has a dust collector with one-touch separation system and a semi-permanent washable HEPA filter.

Germany

Ludwig

Ludwig Leuchten KG

Frühlingstraße 15
86415 Mering
Tel. +49 8233 387-0
Fax +49 8233 387-200
zen@ludwig-leuchten.de
www.ludwig-leuchten.de

Founded in 1949, Ludwig Leuchten KG has grown to become a company well known for superior quality and design. The company's development and reputation began when one of the directors recognised the need to combine excellent product design with dependable function.

Alexander Ludwig believes design satisfies a variety of criteria: one of these is certainly function. But design also says a great deal about competence in a field characterised by standard products that seem to become more and more similar. Good design communicates the difference between conventional work and quality craftsmanship. Ordinary luminaires appear interchangeable and their manufacturers have to compete with low price products. Without design as a marketing tool, it is significantly more difficult to draw attention to the high quality and technical expertise that is in every single luminaire.

In the light of the quickening pace of technological development and innovation, there is another important aspect for the head of design at the family company: looking at a

LED S1: Design by Prof. G. Flohr, Dresden, 2000. LED S1 is the abstraction of a desk luminaire. Graphic, functional, unobtrusive, uncompromising. The luminaire arm and body, both made of enamelled aluminium, are mounted on a safety glass base. The arm can be rotated through 360 degrees. The horizontally and vertically adjustable head is also made of aluminium and fitted with the LED board.
Design Awards 2001: best selection: office design, Design Zentrum Nordrhein Westfalen (Germany) / Office Product Design in the category best lighting, FX International Interior Design Awards

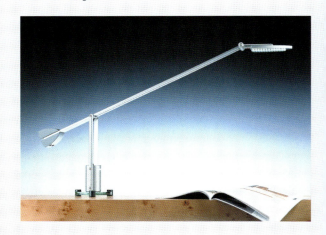

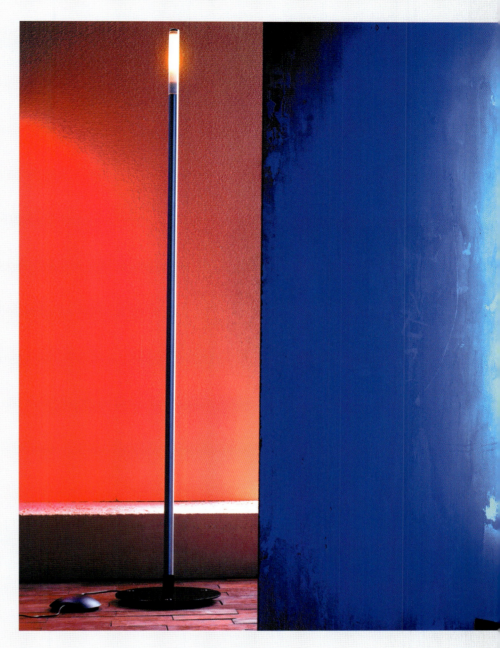

product as a whole. Discriminating design is the thing, in the final analysis, that endures. Design means the opportunity to make history. Ergonomics is the guiding hand in product development. What is pleasing to the eye must also be good for the eye. Besides allowing good visual perception, a luminaire must also satisfy and excite subjective sensibilities. Consolidating these two design objectives is not an easy task for Alexander Ludwig and his team of in-house and external designers. During development, the allure of brilliant design must frequently be forfeited in the face of technological necessities. The primary task is thus to maintain a subtle balance between form and function.

NUR: Design by P. Holzamer and R. Hahn, 2000. Merely a rod – a thin vertical line, at the end of which light emerges: this was the initial inspiration for the NUR design. NUR is a floor-standing luminaire. Its austere purity rejects the trendy and commonplace – the NUR is discreet without being banal. NUR is fitted with a 90 W low-voltage halogen lamp. The luminaire's aluminium head holds a white coated glass tube. The luminaire tube itself is constructed of stove enamelled aluminium, the base is made of powder coated sheet steel.
Design Award 2001: best selection: office design, Design Zentrum Nordrhein Westfalen (Germany)

The TUBE: Design by J. Riedel, 1994 The TUBE is a lighting system not only for foyers, museums, galleries, display windows and showrooms but also for the home. The individual components are easy to change and adapt to different situations. The housing is white painted recyclable aluminium. Fully recyclable opal and blue PMMA has been used for the decorative stripes and effect masks. All the products are equipped with an electronic switching device or dimmer. Wall-mounted, hanging and standard lamps are available.

Design Awards 1995: Red Dot for High Design Quality, Design Zentrum Nordrhein Westfalen (Germany) / Nominated for Bundespreis Produktdesign 1995

This task also means ensuring that resources are used efficiently. Intelligent use of the right luminaire and technical peripherals is a significant contribution to sensible energy consumption – an issue that is not necessarily a hindrance to design work. Innovations in illumination technology, such as the light emitting diode, have tapped new opportunities in the field of luminaire design.

Ludwig Leuchten has succeeded in bringing these aspects together, as demonstrated by their collection of design awards. Still, awards alone are not the determining criteria of good design: it is the acclaim from customers on the luminaire market that convinces Ludwig Leuchten that the company is on the right path.

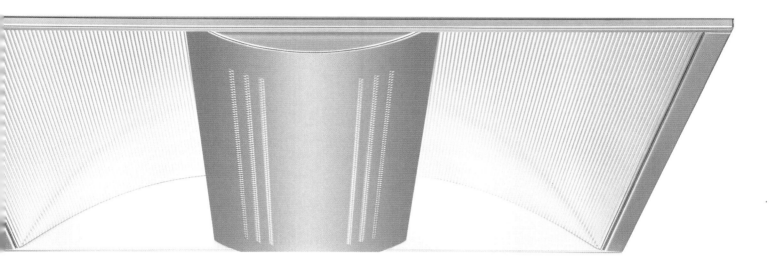

DOJO: Design by R. Rieger, 1995. Dojo is a recessed secondary luminaire with a slotted deflector whose slots are covered by an internal perforated plate. The reflector consists of fluted aluminium plates, giving the luminaire a graceful, light appearance. The square casing and slightly curved deflector are manufactured from sheet steel and, like the aluminium reflector, are painted in RAL 9006 aluminium white. All components of the luminaire are fully recyclable.
Design Award 1996: Red Dot for High Design Quality, Design Zentrum Nordrhein Westfalen (Germany)

MABEG

Germany

MABEG Kreuschner
GmbH & Co. KG

Ferdinand-Gabriel-Weg 10
59494 Soest
Tel. +49 2921 78 06-179
Fax +49 2921 78 06-177
innenraum@mabeg.de
www.mabeg.de

Mabeg, founded in 1921, today optimises living space. This internationally expanding enterprise is a leading producer of items for public spaces, urban furniture and information systems for local public transport services. Over and above this, Mabeg also supplies systems for project furnishing. Mabeg points the way, with crisp concepts and astute designs. The company links up with internationally acclaimed architects and designers to develop modular systems with the functional flexibility and open-endedness to ensure a fitting solution every time. In both indoor and outdoor spaces Mabeg offers orientation, with passenger information products as well as with user-friendly urban furnishings. Its public design offering embraces information systems – static or electronically controlled –, shelters and seating. Mabeg promotes human encounter, with clever solutions for modern project buildings. Its innovative offerings include everything from reception and organisation furniture through ranges with in-built information systems for conferences and presentations to room-in-room modules and exhibition designs.

Profile One is a modular furnishing system that can be used to establish a thematic continuity between the different spaces inside a building. Layouts can be altered and reconfigured at any time, thus ensuring maximum flexibility and design freedom. With a subtle mix of materials and exposed technical systems, the Profile One range creates a highly distinctive environment that sends a strong message to users.

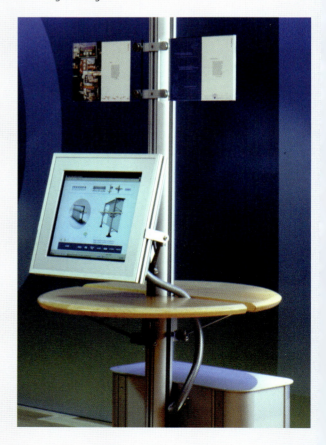

Europa-Center Berlin: The firm that originally designed the Europa-Center in Berlin, architects HPP Hentrich Petschnigg & Partner, has now transformed the structural complex into an office building for our times. Shape has been lent to a new-age working environment that nevertheless preserves the spirit of the original tower, which is listed. One of the floors has been furnished in line with proposals by the architects. The storey is mainly structured by means of a room-divider system based on Profile One. Soest Stools are in place to be sat on where and when required. The conference section is fitted out with components from the P.O.C. Conference and Presentation system.

The Ludwig Erhard Haus, one of Berlin's architectural landmarks, was completed in 1997. On a 22,000 m² site office, exhibition, conference and restaurant facilities have been made available by the architect Nicholas Grimshaw for the Chamber of Commerce, the Berlin Stock Exchange and many other users. In this environment Profile One serves as a signage system as well as part of the furnishing concept. A "dumb porter" in the reception area provides visitors with an overview of the building.

Design Awards 2002: Design Prize of the Federal Republic of Germany by Ministry of Economics and Technology / Consolation Prize for Corporate Design and Design Management, Design Prize of the State of Nordrhein-Westfalen by Ministry of Economics, Technology and Transport of the State of Nordrhein-Westfalen (Germany)

Design Awards 2001: FX Interior Design Award 2001 for the Best Product for Public Spaces, FX Interior Design Awards (Great Britain) / Good Design Award 2001, The Chicago Athenaeum: Museum of Architecture and Design (USA) / red dot: best of the best, Design Zentrum Nordrhein Westfalen (Germany)

Italy

Makio Hasuike & Co

Makio Hasuike & Co

Via Pietro Custodi 16/A
20136 Milano
Tel. +39 02 58 10 31 93
Fax +39 02 58 10 23 11
info@makiohasuike.com
www.makiohasuike.com

Makio Hasuike graduated from the University of Arts of Tokyo in 1962 and began his career in Japan. He worked for one year as a designer for Seiko, designing 20 different clocks for the Olympic Games to be held in Tokyo in 1964. In 1963, Makio Hasuike decided to move to Italy and in 1968 he established his own studio in Milan. Since 1996, he has been teaching at the Faculty of Industrial Design at the Politecnico di Milano, as well as being a member of the founding committee for the Master in Strategic Design.

Founded in 1968, the studio of Japanese designer Makio Hasuike is one of the leading industrial design firms in Italy. In more than 30 years of activity Makio Hasuike has developed successful projects for Italian and foreign companies. Makio Hasuike & Co. works in a wide range of design, from high technology instruments and tools to fashion accessories, from small and large household appliances to furniture and home accessories, from graphic design and packaging to exhibition design.

Impronta MH Way, 1986

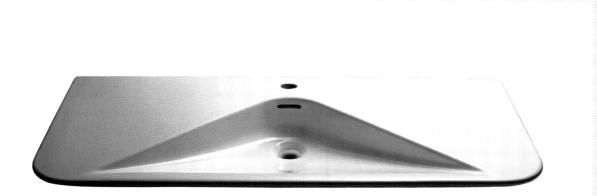

Nirvana Sanitari Pozzi, 1998

Design Awards: Makio Hasuike & Co. has gained worldwide recognition during the years and won many prizes such as Premio Macef / Compasso D'Oro, Triennale / Design Plus, Design Center Stuttgart (Germany) as well as being selected for the Museo del Design at the Triennale di Milano and the Permanent Collection of the Museum of Modern Art, New York.

Client List: Alfi (Germany), Auerhahn (Germany), Ave (Italy), Canados (Italy), Colombo Design (Italy), Del Tongo (Italy), Evolve (Italy), Gaggia (Italy), Gedy (Italy), Merloni Elettrodomestici (Italy), MH WAY (Italy), MTS (Italy), Nestlé (Switzerland), Panasonic (Japan), Piaggio (Italy), Poltrona Frau (Italy), Sanitari Pozzi (Italy), Secco Sistemi (Italy), Seima Exponent (Italy), Venini (Italy), Villeroy & Boch (Germany), WMF (Germany)

Top Star WMF, 1991

Germany

Miele

Miele & Cie. GmbH & Co.

Carl-Miele-Straße 29
33332 Gütersloh
Tel. +49 5241 89-0
Fax +49 5241 89-20 90
info@miele.de
www.miele.de

The cornerstone of Miele's success was laid by the founding fathers, Carl Miele and Reinhard Zinkann. The "Forever better" slogan they coined applies as much today as ever before, epitomising their simple but convincing corporate philosophy. Quality has always taken first place, with all other considerations falling in behind: "Success can only be achieved in the long run if one is totally and utterly convinced of the quality of one's products". By adhering to these principles, the Miele brand has become a synonym for quality, precision and dependability. Miele has always made a point of keeping its promise of quality and, in doing so, has carved out for itself a unique position within its branch of industry.

Miele design aims at highlighting functionality and creating an appearance which is unique and readily recognisable, in short: the visualisation of quality. Miele's success in achieving a synthesis of form and function has resulted in numerous design awards. Prize-winning Miele appliances are on show the world over, not least in the Museum of Modern Art in New York, in the Chicago Athenaeum and in North Rhine-Westphalia's Design Zentrum in Essen.

Miele design stands for simple, self-explanatory controls with easy-to-read text in the user's own language. The owner of a Miele should be able to operate the appliance without first having to read copious instructions.

At the beginning of the 21st century, Miele is a pioneer in many fields of domestic appliance technology. Solid-state engineering has a long tradition at Miele. In 1978, Miele was the first to market with an entire generation of series-produced domestic appliances like washing machines, tumble dryers and dishwashers with microcomputer and sensor-touch controls. 1995 heralded the first machines featuring the Update function. Now, Miele uses fully electronic controls which are developed and produced on site at its own production facilities. Even the unassuming

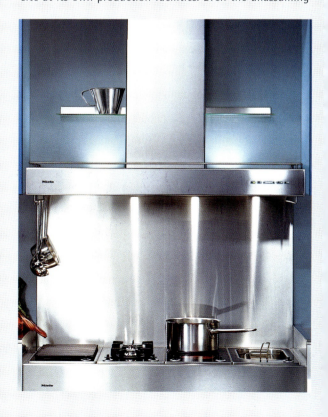

rotary selector switch is high tech – an optical component which does away with mechanical contacts by using tiny beams of light to relay programme selection data to the electronic controls.

From the very outset Miele has cooperated closely with the specialist retail trade. Even in 1899, Miele's first cream separator had to compete with cheaper competitors' products. Consequently there was a need to explain and demonstrate the high standards and features to the farming community. The company founders therefore soon set about finding agricultural equipment suppliers, ironmongers and blacksmiths, whose job was to explain the workmanship and uniqueness to customers in order to improve sales. As a result, 1899 can be seen as the launch of the Miele specialist dealer network.

The Miele brand and the retail trade are an unbeatable team: Miele can boast the most loyal customers and the highest brand repurchase rate. The consumers' confidence in the Miele brand is projected onto its dealers, offering great sales opportunities to brand-conscious customers.

Throughout the company's century-long history, Miele has adhered to the strategy of the founding fathers with tenacity. As a result, Miele's superior products and services have convinced an ever growing circle of consumers. Quality and durability pay out in the long term. To be and remain "forever better" requires a continuous stream of innovations. "Forever better" also means that the generations which follow will continue to improve the company to the competitive gain of consumers and the trade alike.

Molteni

Italy

Molteni & C. S.p.A.

Via Rossini 50
20034 Giussano
Tel +39 0362 35 91
Fax +39 0362 355 170
customer.service@molteni.it
www.molteni.it

Molteni & C. was founded in the early thirties and is based at Giussano. It is one of the few companies in its sector to have an integral production cycle that runs from the purchase of raw materials to the finished product. In the case of wood, in particular, this means accurate quality control, from the choice of timber to the production of the semi-manufactured product, from assembly to finishing – still done manually using the methods of the craftsman to give the products superior quality and a longer life.

Since the 1970s it has been identified with two directions. Firstly by conducting ongoing research in the modular furniture sector and elaborating – with the designs of Luca Meda – a number of solutions for every room in the home – from wardrobes to the living area and study/home office. Modular systems such as 505, 7Volte7 and Pass, to name but a few, are designs in constant evolution, both in technical terms and as regards function and comfort. They have encountered great success and Molteni is considered a leader in this sector.

Since the 1980s in particular, Molteni has offered an extensive collection of individual pieces that combine with the modular furniture to produce a simple, elegant home. Types linked with the collective memory of lifestyles, peculiar to Aldo Rossi designs, were succeeded in the 1990s by pieces such as those designed by Jean Nouvel in which essence is mixed with a high-tech content, a research area that has always been identified with the company.

The company adopts a dualistic approach. On the one hand, it was decided to keep sophisticated craft skills, material know-how, attention to finish, and product personalisation within the company. On the other hand, technological research was developed with constant experiments leading to new solutions. Molteni furniture therefore combines the skills of a longstanding craft tradition with innovative technology that is a great benefit to the user but never ostentatious. Molteni quality is renowned in Italy, where the group is based, but it is also known internationally, because the company exports to the major world markets.

The designers who work with Molteni concur on the idea that furniture must be comfortable but also sturdy with attention to detail and manufactured using prized woods and carefully checked materials. Over and above the charm of each piece, this furniture provides the opportunity to define the lifestyle of the Molteni home. Molteni also works extensively on large contracts, e.g. hotels, museums, ships, chains of shops, hospitals and theatres.

Jei, designed by Studio Cerri & Associati, is a slender and snappy table that makes a strong impact but has a light outline. It was selected for the Compasso d'Oro Milan 2001. It is made of two elements – an elegantly shaped leg in die-cast aluminium and a thin but very solid top with a honeycomb aluminium frame – a totally new application in this field.

Piroscafo, designed by Luca Meda and Aldo Rossi, was conceived as a bookcase or wall unit and has become a classic modern furnishing design. It rests on a high base and its airy division into square modules is marked horizontally at various heights by beam elements – which also close the top. The result is a strong piece of furniture defined like a piece of architecture – one of those designed by the great Italian architects in so many parts of the world from Berlin to Tokyo.

Alfa by Hannes Wettstein is an object of remarkable conception, born from the coupling of just two pieces: one is a back that continues into the rear legs; the other is a seat that extends into the front legs.

Less Years ago Jean Nouvel designed a table conceived as a desk for the Cartier foundation in Paris. Molteni put it into production and it quickly became an icon of that elegantly minimalist design and technological skill that are peculiar to Nouvel.

Germany

mono

mono-Metallwarenfabrik Seibel GmbH

Industriestr. 5
40822 Mettmann
Tel. +49 2104 91 98 -0
Fax +49 2104 91 98 19
mail@mono.de
www.mono.com

Wilhelm Seibel founded the Seibel Britannia Goods Factory in 1895. In 1911 the first branch factory, Hessische Metallwerke Gebr. Seibel, was opened. The company attained global recognition in 1936 with its Olympia cutlery produced specially for the Olympic Village in Berlin. Under the leadership of Herbert Seibel, a grandson of the founder, the company was steered in the late 1950s towards design-orientated products, thus securing the future of Hessische Metallwerke. For generations, mono, based in Mettmann, Germany, has been producing cutlery and table accessories crafted to perfection and aesthetically timeless.

For over 40 years mono has been developing products with designers, and for almost the same period of time it has been the recipient of numerous worldwide awards and citations from design centres and museums, and the publishing house form dedicated a monograph in its series on Design Classics to the mono cutlery designed by Professor Peter Raacke. One unusual honour came from the German Post Office in its special postage stamp series "Design in Germany", in which the mono is shown as one of the most successful examples of contemporary tabletop design. Continuing the commitment to this enduring and successful tradition, the mono company maintains its position as a visionary enterprise. The goal continues to be to create valuable objects for daily use that in turn set new milestones for the enhancement of the quality of life.

gemiini tea service: Mikaela Dörfel created this unusual tea service combining porcelain and stainless steel in 1993. Clearly defined lines, a high degree of functionality and some noteworthy details: the teapot handle, which holds the lid in place when pouring, the precisely fitting strainer insert, and the cantilevered teapot warmer with the elevated candle. The teacups are stackable, with the metal ring serving as stacking guide.

mono-a cutlery: mono-a is the quintessential design of the mono cutlery family. Designed in 1959 by Professor Peter Raacke, it continues to stand for the purist's definition of form and function. mono-a is considered a classic, and has received numerous domestic and international awards. Today, mono-a is known as the best selling German cutlery of the post-war era.

Germany

Niessing

Gebr. Niessing GmbH & Co

Butenwall 117
48691 Vreden
Tel. +49 25 64 300-0
Fax +49 25 64 300-100
service@niessing.com
www.niessing.com

Niessing is a jewellery manufacturer who designs and distributes contemporary jewellery. The company was founded in 1873 by master goldsmith Hermann Niessing in Vreden, Germany. The production of wedding rings and devotional objects was the main objective in the beginning. In the 1950s Niessing was reshaped into a modern manufacturer of wedding rings; in the 1970s the company started producing jewellery. The pursuit of the design strategy has led to the creation of a jewellery collection which, in both its kind and its scope, has achieved a unique position on the market. Niessing has used continuity and innovation to make itself a name for its range of products on the international market.

The uniqueness of Niessing's product assortment results in part from the connections between its minimalist formal idiom and its high quality, but above all from the fact that each jewellery theme is invariably based on a single clear idea – a logical thought which can be clearly formulated and articulated. Nothing is arbitrary or accidental. Each theme is precisely worked out. Whatever is extraneous or merely decorative is summarily eschewed so that nothing can conceal the idea, the underlying and all-important thought.

The product itself provides for a recognisable, stimulating and convincing appearance. This is what the company calls "communicative aesthetics". The basic function of jewellery is to give its wearers opportunities to express and underline their feelings and personalities.

The pursuit of a logical design strategy has led to a number of international design awards such as:

Design Awards 2001: red dot: best of the best for Shape It, Design Zentrum Nordrhein Westfalen (Germany)

Design Awards 1999: Busse Longlife Design Award for the Niessing Ring®, Busse Design (Germany) / iF Product Design Award for Braided Jewellery, Industrie Forum Design (Germany)

Design Awards 1998: Red Dot for the Highest Design Quality for Braided Jewellery, Design Zentrum Nordrhein Westfalen (Germany)

Design Awards 1997: Prize of Honour for Product Design for Wedding Ring System, Design Prize of the State of Nordrhein-Westfalen by Ministry of Economics, Technology and Transport of the State of Nordrhein-Westfalen (Germany)

Niessing Ring®

Braided Jewellery: Braided bands have been around for 5000 years. But one made purely of gold is extraordinary. Forged bands are rigid and bend easily. Chains, with their loose links, do not keep the required shape. Designer Timo Küchler has found the golden mean for Niessing: the finest handicraft combined with the latest technology.
A band is cut from a metal sheet and braided into a circle. An infinite loop apparently made of two or three bands results. The solution: a computer-calculated model of the curvature, a laser for precise cutting out, and a special gold alloy, which enables the band to be given an exact pretension. The material can bend without kinking. And at the same time, it is only a quarter of a millimetre thick. Less is not possible. More would distort the smooth elegance. The edges are rounded off.

A substantial piece of jewellery in precious metal, and yet extremely light. A balance of material, strength and flexibility. A fabric which gets noticed; not too much and not too little. And always in motion.

ideo – 2001 Tokyo Motor Show: The exterior and interior of ideo have been executed in an advanced and user-friendly design. ideo is a medium for connecting the passenger compartment to the outside world. The objective of this concept car is to enable occupants to enjoy communicating by giving them efficient access to the innumerable information in the world.

Quest concept – 2002 Detroit Auto Show: The Quest Concept is a bold departure from traditional minivan design. It features a long, sleek cabin with a flowing beltline gesture, a unique wraparound glass treatment and to emphasise its performance capabilities, tyres pushed out to the corners. Quest Concept includes a power operated bi-fold tailgate that operates in a limited amount of space and a glass roof.

Japan

Nissan

Nissan Motor Co., Ltd.

17-1, Ginza 6-chome,
Chuo-ku
Tokyo 104-8023, Japan
Tel. +81 3 55 65-21 41
Fax +81 3 35 46-26 69
www.nissan-global.com

Nissan was established in 1933 to manufacture and sell small Datsun passenger cars and auto parts. Committed to designing and engineering vehicles that are fully satisfying to customers, Nissan addresses a host of issues related to automobile use, ranging from traffic safety to global environmental concerns.

Nissan is engaged in corporate activities on a global scale, operating 20 manufacturing companies in 16 countries around the world and marketing Nissan vehicles in 191 countries. In March 1999, Nissan and Renault signed a comprehensive alliance agreement aimed at strengthening Nissan's financial position and at the same time achieving profitable growth for both companies.

Nissan and Renault collaborate as global partners while each company maintains its own unique identity. Since Nissan announced its 3-year Nissan Revival Plan in October 1999, it has been promoting various activities to reestablish the Nissan brand in a swift manner. As the management aims at continuous growth and development for Nissan, the responsibility and importance of design has been emphasised.

The company developed and introduced 15 concept cars from the Paris motor show in September of 2000 to the Detroit motor show in January of 2002 while presenting 9 new models to the market, such as the Primera and Micra for Europe, and the Altima and 350Z for the USA.

αT – 2001 Detroit Auto Show: The αT concept's appearance may be a little startling to those who have come to view trucks as sedans with an open trunk. Following Nissan's tradition of building authentic, hard working, hard playing pickups, the αT's design appeals to the true truck lover's desire for a big, powerful, aggressive looking vehicle with more than just a little edge to it. The αT exterior features a massive front grille, bumper and headlights, scooped bonnet, an aggressive 4-door body with butterfly open doors for easy access, a sharply sloped A-pillar, and unique glass panel roof treatment with personalised opening sections.

350Z is designed to impress viewers at first sight. This Z embodies many new features for a sports car, all of which have been implemented in high quality. The Z is very fluid and relaxed, from the curve of the door cut to the freeness and movement of the glass. It looks fast, but not just in a straight line. It is a simple yet exacting design, which gives the Z a polished feeling.

Primera: A graceful yet dynamic "monoform silhouette" integrates the elegance of Japanese aesthetics in a stable stance. The Primera will be the next generation mainstream benchmark to provide customers with an optimum blend of excellent driving performance and ride comfort.

Design Awards 2001/2002: Good Design Award 2001 in the category Gold Prize (Japan) / Japan Car Design Award 2001, Golden Marker / Auto Color Awards 2002 (Japan) Judges` Special Awards (Luminous Red), Technical Division (Silica Brass)

Altima is a luxury sports sedan, focusing on three key factors: design, performance and space. The Altima features an aggressive design of arched upper body on the wedged shape lower body with high waistline and clear character line. Integrated front and rear bumpers create a sleek streamlined silhouette. The modern and comfortable design optimises the interior space for harmony between the driver and car (North American Car of The Year in 2002).

Tokyo Motor Show Booth: For the enhancement of Nissan brand identity, the Nissan motor show booth is designed to articulate the attractiveness of motor vehicles. As the prevailing colour in the Nissan Ginza gallery is white, all unnecessary elements were eliminated to create a place where the audience concentrates on display models. Lighting design ensures maximum effect to attract the audience; it succeeds in stimulating their curiosity about the inner side of the booth by blocking out any visual noise from outside. At overseas motor shows, Japanese DNA was emphasised while Nissan brand taste was emphasised much more at domestic motor shows.

Ginza Showroom: The concept of Nissan Ginza Gallery is "Imagination Crossing". Nissan aims at providing customers with a "space medium" where they can experience Nissan as an imagination factory through the products. All unnecessary elements were eliminated. It is a place where people concentrate on cars and cars appear to be the best they can be for true appreciation.

For the establishment of a globally consistent design identity, Nissan Design has been expanding its activities beyond car design. The approach is that design responsibility does not end with the completion of a vehicle, but only when the company delivers the brand message to their customers. The design team therefore also works on space design such as the Ginza Gallery and the Nissan motor show booth.

Germany

nya nordiska textiles GmbH

An den Ratswiesen
D-29451 Dannenberg
Fon + 49 5861 80 9-0
Fax + 49 5861 80 9-10
nya@nya.com
www.nya.com

Nya Nordiska

The textile company nya nordiska was founded by Heinz Röntgen over 35 years ago. His activities now focus primarily on the design of new products, with the management functions increasingly passing to his wife Diete Hansl-Röntgen and four children. nya nordiska – a classical family business.

The company sells through specialist dealers in Germany, other European countries and worldwide, supported by over forty agencies. There are subsidiaries in Como, Paris and London. The business has its head office in northern Germany, housed in a half-timbered factory building which will soon be 150 years old, and an ultra-modern glass and concrete structure. A contrast which reflects the principles of nya nordiska's product philosophy.

nya nordiska is always striving to produce contemporary yet timeless design, which for many years now has been almost a trademark of the nya nordiska collection.

Bijoux: The chemical fibre industry is extending the textile design horizons, with more and more new creations. Super fine little bands of foil, steamed, printed, dyed, arriving after a trip through the world of ores; gold and silver, pyrites and copper and even cinnabar. Then finally ground and polished as proof that high gloss can have a deep glow. Always a subject, but often the subject for stage appearances. Staging a production at home? It's already underway!
Decorating fabric by Heinz Röntgen – 50% polyester, 50% polyester-metal; 30 g/m^2.

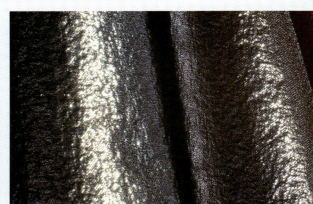

Crivello Sheers: Very thin stretch – resistant beam threads with right – threaded technique counterbalanced to the point constitute a solid bonding basis for proportionally extremely voluminous brightly finished threads in the weft.
The almost unreal drop in volume creates an apparently insoluble problem. The thrill of experimenting and technical self – will has resulted in a fabric creation that practically demands that it be used to great effect. Design Heinz Röntgen – 70% polyester, 30% viscose; 30 g/m².

Impulsa: Surge within electricity? Behavioural impetus within psychology or imaginative push through sailing? A bit of all this is what the spinnaker fabric has with the touch of paper and with a surrealistic design Impulsa, cut by the latest laser techniques. Design Heinz Röntgen – 100% nylon/polyamide, 60 g/m².

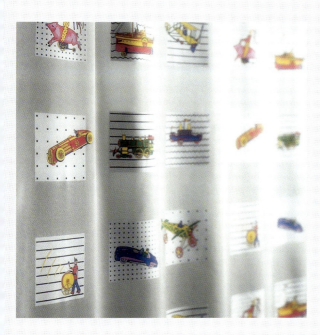

Design-Concept Tusca and Tuscany: Tusca is an example of the metallic look. No one is talking about sheet metal, this is putting utopia into practice with "metal" in a textile. Extreme fibre mix and Jacquard technique produce metallic impressions, tamed and shimmering. By changing the weave, forming diamonds, a composition arises: Tuscany. Design Heinz Röntgen – 40% polyester, 30% cotton, 15% viscose, 15% polypropylene; 350 g/m^2.

Racing-car is a decorating fabric. An attempt to translate images of past enjoyment into the modern age, capturing all the "joie de vivre" and "naiveté" of former times on the fabric of the present. Almost automatically, the implementation becomes a journey through the variety of textile materials and techniques. Design: Design-Team nya nordiska. 59% polyester, 41% cotton; 30 g/m^2.

Italy

O Luce

O Luce s.r.l.

via Cavour, 52
20098 San Giuliano
Milanese - Milano
Tel. +39 02 98 49 14 35
Fax +39 02 98 49 07 79
info@oluce.com
www.oluce.com

Established in 1945 in Milan by Giuseppe Ostuni, OLuce is the oldest Italian lighting design company that is still active today. O Luce had played host to the young Joe Colombo in the early nineteen-sixties and he produced a range of items that are still in its catalogue. In the early nineteen-seventies a new and important era began at O Luce, coinciding with the transfer of ownership from Ostuni to the Verderi family and dominated by one of the great masters of Italian design: Vico Magistretti. For many years Magistretti was Art Director and Chief Designer of the company, conferring upon it his unmistakable stamp and leaving a legacy of worldwide recognition. Kuta, Lester, Nara, Idomeneo, Pascal, Dim, Sonora, Snow, and especially Atollo even became a sort of icon, a graphic silhouette that immediately rendered the concept of a "lamp".

Colombo 626: Designed in 1972 by Joe Colombo, Colombo 626 was the first indoor halogen light to appear on the market. Floor lamp with dimmer giving direct and indirect light, lacquered steel base, chromium-plated or black lacquered stem, height adjustable reflector in lacquered aluminium.

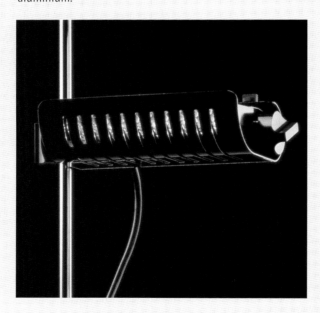

If the manufacturer, as is the case of OLuce, is one of the historic names of Italian design, a catalogue can only live like this, nurtured on tradition and experience so as to move on towards new definitions. Moreover, Italian design has always developed along these lines, constantly endeavouring to surpass itself and constantly supported by an extraordinary business organisation, by a refined technological wealth and above all by each and every person's unfailing passion for this work.

In the late nineteen-nineties, Oluce also proved capable of opening its doors to new Italian and European designers so that they could contribute their knowledge of the most recent trends. All of them, with the experience of the company behind them, were left entirely free to express themselves in their own specific language: the poetic minimalism of Marta Laufani and Marco Romanelli, the disruptive energy of Toni Cordero and the Campana brothers, the dry words of Hans Peter Weidmann and Till Leeser, the expressive research of Stefano Casciani and Ferdi Giardini and the concise elegance of Sebastian Bergne and Francesco Rota.

Design Awards: Many Honour Award Assignments for the International Competition "ADI Compasso d'Oro" recently conferred for the lamps Nuvola 195 and Lanterna 477 in 2001 / Compasso d'Oro ADI for Atollo lamp in 1979 / Compasso d'Oro ADI for Spider 291 lamp in 1967 / Gold Medal at the Triennale Milano for Colombo 281 lamp in 1964 / International Design Award, American Institute of Interior Designers Chicago 1968 for Coupè 3321 lamp / International Design Award, American Institute of Interior Designers Chicago 1970 for Spring lamp

O Luce's lamps appear in the most important museums of the world. Museum of Modern Art, New York / Philadelphia Museum of Art, Philadelphia / Kunstgewerbe Museum, Zurich / Museum Die neue Sammlung, Munich / Museum für Kunst und Gewerbe, Hamburg / Kunstmuseum, Düsseldorf / Permanent Collection of Italian Design, Milano Triennale

Atollo became a sort of icon, a graphic silhouette that immediately defined what a lamp should be. Atollo, essentially inimitable though copied around the world, winner of the "Compasso d'Oro" in 1979 and featured in the permanent collections of all the leading design and decorative arts museums – has thus become much more than just a lamp: it is a legend. Its secret probably lies in the geometry of its forms: the cone on the cylinder. All surmounted by the hemisphere.
Table lamp giving direct and diffused light: diffuse in opaline blown Murano glass, direct light with dimmer in the lacquered aluminium version.

O Luce   Hall of Fame   119

Propagandist

Thailand

Propagandist Co. Ltd.

779 /210
Pracharajbumphen Rd.
Samsennoak, Huay kwang
Bangkok / 10320
Tel. +66 2 691-63 31
Fax +66 2 691-34 78
info@propagandaonline.com
www.propagandaonline.com

Propaganda was the beginning of a new era for Thailand's world of product design, established in 1994. Gradually expanding its know-how from graphic design work to become a company that would soon focus solely on designing, Propagandists all shared one goal – to be at the helm of the local design market. The prime motive was to invent new forms, giving each of them a conceptual function.

The ultimate challenge, however, was to present works from Thailand to the global market and eventually push them to the forefront of the international design arena. Propaganda is out to change everyday life by injecting a surge of playfulness into items that would otherwise be regarded as everyday objects. The aim is not simply to be different, but more essentially, to make a difference, transforming what customers have described as "the doldrums" into the stuff of thrilling individualism. Propagandist Co. is a group of designers who distribute their brand mainly through various international trade fairs across the world, including the 'Ambiente' and 'Tendence' in Frankfurt or the 'Maison et Objet' in Paris. The clients come from all over the globe, including Europe and Asia – namely France, Germany, the Netherlands, Belgium, Portugal, Denmark, Norway, Sweden, Finland, Iceland, England, Russia, Korea, Japan, Indonesia and Hong Kong. With their relentless determination to become the best at what they do, this team of designers has won many awards. In Chicago, there were three Good Design Awards for two years running – one in 2000 and two in 2001. These awards from the Chicago Athenaeum, Museum of Architecture and Design, were in honour of the Saltepper, a two in one salt and pepper shaker by Chaiyut Plypetch under the housewares/tabletop category.

Another winning creation by the same designer is the magnetic bottle opener, the Shark. In the same year, Kunlanath Sornsriwichai also reaped another award for the Dish Up, a set of tableware items under the houseware category. All these three award-winning designs are on display at the museum's permanent design collection.

Saltepper, 2000

Shark, 2001

Dish up, 2001

Ap-peel, 2002

The designers are the foundation and heart of the company. Their flair for combining local elements with the typically Thai "kee len", playful attitude is what delineates Propaganda designs and is what has become the company's trademark. Propagandist Co. is passionate in its approach.: "These designers are the heart and soul of our company and with them, we as a company will endeavour to achieve our goals through perseverance and faith in our homemade talents."

Design Awards 2002: red dot for "Ap-peel" fruit bowl and knife, Design Zentrum Nordrhein Westfalen (Germany) / Good Design Award for "Ap-peel" fruit bowl and knife and for "Melting Bulb" table lamp, Museum of Architecture and Design Chicago (USA) / Good Design Award 2002, for "Ap-peel" fruit bowl and knife (Japan)

Rado

Switzerland

Rado Watch Co. Ltd.

Bielstrasse 45
2543 Lengnau
Tel. +41 32 655-61 11
Fax +41 32 655-61 12
www.rado.com

Being different means walking a different path. It means being a pioneer. At Rado this kind of pioneering is a tradition. And the goal is always the same: to bring form and function into harmony; to create designs that are ahead of their time – in materials that will outlast it.

As long as forty years ago, Rado was already breaking new ground as the first watch company to use hard materials and refine them for aesthetic purposes. In 1962 the company in Lengnau astonished the watch-making world with a new invention: the world's first scratch-proof watch – made from an unlikely-looking powder, which was developed by Rado's engineers to create an ultra-hard carbide metal that stays always beautiful. While other brands use traditional materials such as gold, brass or steel, Rado prefers materials like carbide-based hard metals, sapphire crystal, high-tech ceramics and high-tech diamond. Over the decades Rado has worked with a number of innovative and dynamic high-tech specialists to build a unique fund of know-how in scratchproof watch design. This know-how is based on 30 patents and has made Rado the world's undisputed leading maker of scratchproof watches.

The creation of Rado's carbide-based hard metal involves a costly process: the raw material, consisting of titanium carbide powder or tungsten carbide powder, is pressed into blanks under a pressure of 1000 bar. These are compacted in a sintering furnace at 1450 degrees Celsius into their final form. A number of other processes also take place before final polishing using diamond powder, thus creating the incomparable brilliance that is typical of Rado – a brilliance that contributes to Rado's own unique language of form and sets it apart from the competition.

The raw material for the industrial manufacture of sapphire crystal is once again a powder: extremely pure aluminum oxide powder. This is crystallized in a Verneuil kiln at 2050 degrees Celsius into a nugget of sapphire. The nugget is first cut into disks using highly specialised diamond cutters. A number of additional processes are used for calibration of the raw disks, abrasion to the correct shape, surface grinding, Biseau cutting, faceting and polishing. The final result is the crystal-clear protective shield that will protect the surface of a Rado from scratches forever.

Completely new and yet perfectly true to the brand philosophy – this idea, underlining all Rado developments, is here embodied by the successful 'Ceramica' model. In the Rado design lab, new creations do not simply come from the designer's drawing board, nor are they churned out of a development engineer's computer. They are the result of a constant dialog in which the designer adjusts the technical ideas and the engineer contributes design suggestions.

With the company's typical inventive spirit, Rado is constantly looking for new, harder materials which are even more skin-friendly. The team of researchers came up with high-tech ceramics, a material that has already proved itself in outer space. Used in the form of a heat shield, it protects spacecraft on re-entry into the atmosphere from the burning-up that would otherwise be inevitable.
Rado high-tech ceramics brings together not only characteristics such as scratch resistance and extreme toughness, it is also particularly skin- friendly and anti-allergenic. The stages in the manufacturing process are similar to those in the hard-metal process: microscopically fine zirconium-oxide powder with a granule size of approx. 1/1000th of a millimetre is pressed into shape and compacted by sintering at 1450 degrees Celsius to make scratch-proof ceramic parts. More recently Rado has often also used the injection moulding process. This makes it possible to manufacture more complex shapes with the utmost precision.

The Rado 'Ovation': The watch and strap flow smoothly into one another, creating a harmonious whole. A clear language of form in scratchproof high-tech ceramics.

Rado's researchers have never given up their ceaseless quest for the ultimate hardness of diamond. Despite the successful use of hard metal and high-tech ceramics, their tireless search has continued and still continues for new and harder materials.

Rado's newest and most revolutionary invention shows how close those engineers have come to the goal of perfection: high-tech diamond. To create this unparalleled material, diamonds are ground to powder and exposed to a temperature of 1500 degrees Celsius and an almost unimaginable pressure of 50,000 bar. Sintering this powder together with a hard-metal substrate creates Rado high-tech diamond. This remarkable milestone will secure Rado's technological lead for years to come.

Randstad

Netherlands

Randstad Holding nv

Diemermere 25
1112 TC Diemen
Tel. +31 20 569-51 75
Fax +31 20 569-56 32
www.randstad.com

Halfway through the sixties there was no corporate style culture to speak of in the Netherlands. The Dutch manufactured and sold soap, petrol or coffee on the basis of traditionally established reputations. Branding and corporate image were still vague concepts. Here and there a flourishing gold-lettered 'Royal Warrant Holder' reminded people of a glorious past. Any other activity related to the public image of a company – including advertising – was met with suspicion. Image building was pie in the sky. This, then, was the market in which, practically simultaneously, two new companies were founded.

In the centre of Amsterdam a group of young designers set up the first Dutch multidisciplinary design company under the name of Total Design. It quickly made a name for itself with its sober, systematic approach to typography, product development and communication. Total Design became associated with important clients who recognised the value of an integrated approach to design: petroleum company PAM for instance, the Stedelijk Museum Amsterdam and various public organisations to name but a few. By the time Total Design celebrated its 20th anniversary in 1983, styles and tastes might have changed, but like no other design company Total Design had made its mark.

In 1960, barely a couple of kilometres beyond the Amsterdam canals, in the neighbouring town of Amstelveen, economist Frits Goldschmeding founded his company in another relatively unexplored market. The early beginnings of Randstad, which he founded whilst still at college, can be traced to his thesis on the phenomenon of temporary labour.

Now, more than 40 years on, the Randstad Group is one of the largest international temporary employment organisations and market leader in the Netherlands, Belgium, Germany and the south-eastern United States. Randstad Holding specialises in finding solutions in the field of flexible workforces and human resource services, with group companies in countries throughout Europe, the USA and Canada.

Randstad's beginnings were humble but as early as the sixties it expanded its activities throughout the Netherlands, followed by subsidiaries in Belgium, Germany, France and Britain. In 1967 the founder met the Amsterdam Design Company for the first time in what would be a long and fruitful relationship. Temping was not a fashionable word in those days. Mediation for temporary office employment and administrative work was not the order of the day, especially not in the Netherlands. Randstad had a different mission and to this day projects the same message. Temporary employment is not a cynical coupling of incidental labour demand to random supply but gives both parties the opportunity to develop. This is how Randstad opts for continuity, in its own organisation as well as in the relationship it has with clients, temporary employees, its own workforce and the society in which it operates.

Calendar 2002

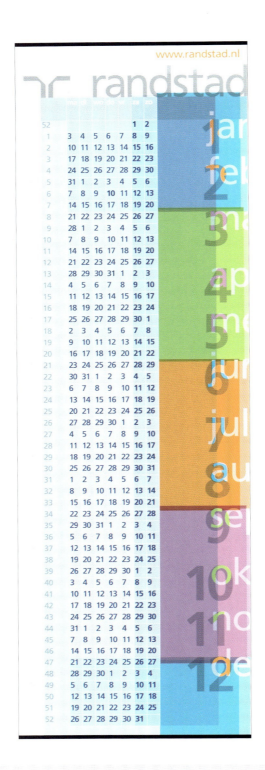

Calendar 2002

Randstad recognises the importance of the interdependent role it plays in society. It realises it depends on society, but is furthermore astutely aware that the reverse also applies: Randstad influences society. Randstad strives to act on behalf of all parties involved, always basing its decision-making process on three core values, 'to know, to serve and to trust'. In an interview given in 1988, Goldschmeding remarked that these concepts had not yet crystallised when he first met with Total Design for discussions on a new house style. 'We started out with hardcore numerical analysis, yet eventually the one central question remained: What are the core elements of human communication?'

This is where the concepts 'to know, to serve and to trust' stem from . In collaboration with designer Ben Bos and his team at Total Design, Randstad introduced a design in 1967 that is still considered exemplary today. Unlike all other print and stick-and-post work that had been produced up till then, this was clear, open, humane and with an capacity to survive. Alterations to the house style over the past thirty years have been marginal. Some new typefaces were introduced and the colour spectrum increased and refined, but when in the mid-nineties Randstad decided to commission different design companies, the essential design, the emblem of their public image, actually hardly changed.

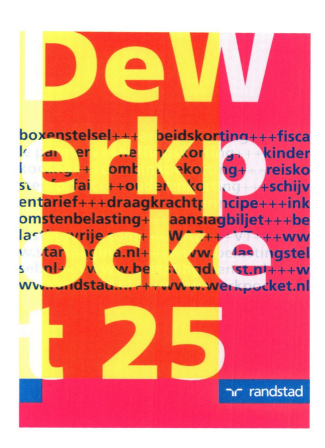

The Workpocket 2002

The key to their house style success is that the graphic design and the philosophy of the organisation are interwoven. It is for this very reason that the 'Randstad case' became a cause célèbre in the history of European design.

The house style is not so much about a logo or about the layout of an application form, but is rooted in the service-minded character of the organisation as a whole, and hence proliferates in both the external and internal communication of Randstad. It is impossible to separate the logo from the company's philosophy, or to separate the philosophy from the logo. Both convey the same identity.

Consequently, when Randstad approached Wim Quist for the design of a new head office the brief simply outlined that what they wanted was the quality and service they strive for to be translated into 'concrete and stone'. House Style has always been one of the core values of the company. Together with the designers and marketing managers from different subsidiaries, Randstad's Board of Directors determines the specific house styles. Design plays a key role in the development and utilisation of all of Randstad's facilities. Various design companies produce brochures, backpacks, promotional materials, company gifts such as the classic Bruno Ninaber ruler (part of Randstad office stationery), calendars, agendas (Studio Dumbar, Eden), commercials, annual reports and several company magazines. Services are not a clear, tangible product and it is the people who constitute what Randstad stands for. The product design should support Randstad's workforce in an efficient, recognisable way. It is these products after all that are always distinguishable, like the buildings and interiors of Randstad offices.

These days this package includes the website, designed by Mediamatic, a design company and publisher located in the Amsterdam harbour. For years Randstad has been commissioning Dutch photographers for its Work project. Leading and up-and-coming photographers have gained their place in the collection. Initially these photographs served a practical purpose only: in offices, magazines, and advertising campaigns. In 1988 it was decided to form a collection around this commissioned work that could be seen as a companion piece to the Randstad art collection.

This was the start of a collection that includes all kinds of artwork related to the theme of Work. Parts of the collection are exhibited at different locations, including the Randstad offices themselves. The photographic images are also still used for the Randstad office agendas, as well as for the different marketing products. This is because in spite of Randstad's enormous growth over the past 40 years, its basic sense of continuity has never wavered.

Paperclipholder 2002

Samsung

Korea

Samsung
Electronics Co., Ltd.

Samsung Main Building
250-2ga, Taepyung-ro
Chung-gu, Seoul
Tel. +82 2 751-33 55
www.sec.co.kr

Corporate Design Center
14F, Joong-ang ilbo Bldg.,
7 Soonhwa-Dong, Choong-
Ku, Seoul
Korea 100-759
Tel. +82 2 750-92 96
Fax +82 2 750-94 25
www.samsungelectronics.com

Samsung was founded in Taegu in 1938 by Byung-Chull Lee. Samsung produced and sold goods in the region and carried on trade with China and Manchuria. In 1947 Samsung moved to Seoul, the economic centre of Korea, and strengthened its position. In 1969 Samsung Electronics was founded and is today a global leader in the manufacture and supply of innovative electronics solutions – which in turn is part of the Samsung Group, one of the world's largest companies with over 230,000 employees in 63 countries. With a proven pedigree in the development and manufacture of electronics for commercial and domestic applications, Samsung Electronics is a world leader in many fields including the computer memory market, with a market share of 30%. 13,000 staff are committed to the development of cutting-edge technology to ensure that Samsung Electronics is at the forefront of research into data and voice communications.

In order to become the leader of the digital convergence era, Samsung Electronics manages four strategic businesses in the following fields: Home, Mobile, Office Network and Core Components. As digital convergence becomes an integral part of our everyday life, Samsung Electronics practises "Digital- ε Company" to accelerate future business opportunities and innovation in management. It converges and networks technology, products, and business by restructuring its business portfolio and strengthening its design ability, to come up with a product renewal that reflects the needs of the digital convergence era.

Samsung Electronics will network core components such as memory chips, system-LSI and LCDs as well as A/V, computers, telecommunication devices, home appliances and other stand-alone products into a total solution for the digital convergence era.

The company's senior management has clearly realised the value of design for business success, as evidenced by Samsung Group chairman Kun Hee Lee's proclamation: "Intellectual assets will determine a company's value in the 21st century, the 'era of culture'. The age when companies simply sell products is over. In the new era, enterprises have to sell their corporate philosophy and culture. An enterprise's most vital assets lie in its design and other creative capabilities. I believe the ultimate winners in 21st century will be determined by these skills." Based on its design philosophy "Balance of Reason and Feeling", Samsung Corporate Design Center is creating distinguished products, but also new experiences and values that exceed customers' expectations. Furthermore, it is constantly seeking new business opportunities to realise the company's long-term vision and position itself as the Core Creation Center. According to the CEO's conviction, the company has determined to pursue a design-driven management policy.

Portable Microwave Oven AC/DC MWO: Camping may never be the same if this concept becomes a reality. The DC-operated portable microwave oven for minivans, SUVs and campers would have all the features of a standard oven, but be durable and light enough to carry. The durable yet unique design language expresses its functionality while offering an appropriate fashion statement.

Digital Network Refrigerator SR-N759 CSC: What will the refrigerators of the future be like? How about a refrigerator that detects the shelf life of food and informs the consumer about it, or one that automatically displays a list of items stored in the fridge on the door? The Digital Network refrigerator SR-N759 CSC is Samsung's first step into the future. Equipped with internet capability, a videophone and a TV, this refrigerator will be at the centre of the home of tomorrow.

GSM Mobile Phone SGH-T100 is the first GSM mobile phone to be built with a TFT LCD display. The futuristic, aerodynamic design embodies the state-of-the-art technology applied in the phone. The ergonomic design breaks away from the typical chunky body and improves the grip on the phone.

The folder-style phone has a large colour LCD display showing 128x160 pixels. Still, it fits comfortably within a palm, which makes it highly portable. Users can pick any wallpaper they want for the TFT LCD display. In addition to the high resolution TFT LCD display, users can also enjoy 16-poly ring tone melodies to express their unique individuality.

In addition to the Chief Design Officer overseeing the company's design-related activities and more than 300 inhouse designers developing the company's product designs, Samsung has also established the Design Research Institute dedicated to research and new business development activities regarding lifestyle, user behaviour, colour, material and user interface. Moreover, in order to carry out the global design strategy, Samsung has set up a global design network with key sites in the USA (San Francisco, Los Angeles), United Kingdom (London) and Japan (Tokyo). Starting in 1993, the company pursued a unique policy called 'Design Membership' to nurture prospective designers with outstanding potential and actively support joint research activities with academia. Furthermore, the Samsung Art and Design Institute constantly helps designers to be armed with a global perspective and advanced creativity.

Portable DVD Player DVD-L100 is only 23.5 mm thick, has a 10" LCD screen, comes with a built-in Memory Stick slot, and allows users to enjoy music as well as still pictures. DVD-L100 is the perfect entertainment solution for a family who enjoy outdoor life at weekends and on holidays. Children can watch movies in the back seat while the parents drive. All family members are able to enjoy movies, music, and still pictures together in any place thanks to the larger screen. The delicate magnesium finishing and the corrugation design on the surface render the images of rigidity and high-quality. The slimness of 23.5mm maximises portability and the user-friendly interface enables anyone and everyone to operate the device, optimising user convenience.

40-inch LCD TV LT40A1 is the largest LCD screen TV in the world. This TV has the fastest response time of 12~16 ms, the highest brightness at 500:1, the highest contrast ratio at 600:1, and Ultra Spectacle sound by 3 way 6 speakers for 40" models or 2 way 4 channels for 29" models. Simple and clean design language gives a greater value and enriches digital life with premium style.

Design Awards: Samsung's commitment to good design has resulted in significant recognition both domestically and internationally. Samsung received 73 good design awards from international design competitions such as Industrial Design Excellence Awards in USA, IF Product Design Award, International Forum Design at Hanover (Germany), and G Mark in Japan for last several years. At IDEA, Samsung received 17 major design awards over the last five years, including five awards this year, and tied with Apple for the first place on Business Week's list of Corporate Design Award Winners. Design is now recognised not only as one of the competitive factors, but also as a strategic activity to create a corporate image and to innovate the brand value. This belief on design will develop Samsung's corporate value.

The Family Doctor: The futuristic design and analogy has creative appeal and the detailing of the monitor is refined. The Family Doctor is a friendly pill form home diagnostic concept. One part of the device is ingested while another monitors the results, then feeds those results through a network to the physician. The user can handle emergencies and manage health conditions through the network connecting the service provider, hospital and pharmacy. The network updates medical information and allows video conversations with the family doctor and pharmacist, providing convenience in terms of time and location. The compact size and the capsule-type metaphor enhances portability and also provides an easy to use interface for the elderly and children.

Germany

Schwan Stabilo

**Schwan-Stabilo
Schwanhäußer GmbH & Co.**

Schwanweg 1
90562 Heroldsberg
Tel. +49 911 567-0
Fax +49 911 567-44 44
info@stabilo.com
www.stabilo.com

Schwan-Stabilo Schwanhäusser GmbH & Co. produces and markets a wide range of writing and drawing implements worldwide under the Stabilo brand name. The history of this family business goes back as far as 1855, when the company began producing pencils. Today the Schwan-Stabilo group employs about 2800 people around the world. As well as writing equipment, the three companies also produce and market cosmetic pencils and advertising media. The company can look back on numerous innovations that are still widely used today. With the invention of the "Stabilo Boss" fluorescent marker and its huge international success, it became clear that the classical idea of an efficient writing implement is not in itself enough to satisfy consumers' increasingly specialised needs.

In the Stabilo innovation lab, experts from marketing, technology and design work together in a permanent interdisciplinary process. The innovation lab's aim is to seek out trend-setting themes and use these to develop new product ideas. The Stabilo innovation lab is managed by designers. This allows optimum use to be made of design's classic role as a mediator between various disciplines, and it simplifies the communication of results. By integrating design into development processes early on, design is made to work as a brand identity factor for the company. Every day, millions of people use Stabilo products in offices, in schools and at home. The company views every new Stabilo product as a response to the needs of those people, on both the emotional and the technical level.

Stabilo Boss, 1971 In-house design 1971, redesign 1994 by Ewald Winkelbauer from Winkelbauer-Design, Ludwigsburg. The Stabilo Boss fluorescent marker was developed in 1971 following an idea by Günther Schwanhäusser. On its market launch it was an international innovation both in its function and design – it was the first pen for reading. Its form, evoking a hand-axe, and the Stabilo Boss name, confer on it the attributes of a "wand pen" that is used for taking decisions. Today, two Stabilo Boss fluorescent markers are sold every second around the world – their form and function are still up to date even after more than 30 years.

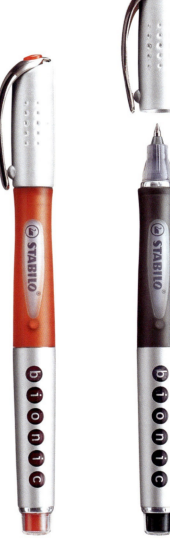

Stabilo 's move the elastic writer, 1999 Design by factor product munich. The Stabilo 's move is an ink fineliner developed primarily for young user groups. Design and materials for the 's move take their inspiration from the basketball scene. At the same time, the ball is a metaphor for the pen's cushioned tip that works like a shock absorber as you write. The voluminous slim-waist barrel is made of soft rubber. It prevents cramp in the writer's hand. The 's move can be attached to a bag or belt with a special cling band, making it easy for others to see.

Stabilo bionic, 2001 Design by Ewald Winkelbauer from Winkelbauer-Design, Ludwigsburg. The Stabilo bionic is notable for the functional interplay of different materials. Ultra high-tech 2-component injection moulding enables a haptically seamless transition with integrated roll-stop. Windows made of transparent materials let you see the replaceable refill cartridge. Translucent colours and muted colours identity carriers for the different writing tips. A fine concave grip pattern facilities taking off and replacing the cap. A technical innovation is the large-sized but still springy metal clip with integrated colour cap.

Germany

Sedus

Sedus Stoll AG

Brückenstraße 15
79761 Waldshut
Tel. +49 7751 84 -0
Fax +49 7751 84 -3 10
info@sedus.de
www.sedus.de

Sedus Stoll AG, founded in 1871, and a public company since 1995 is one of the leading European manufacturers of office seating, conference furniture, healthy back furniture and multipurpose chairs. The company's headquarters and main manufacturing base are located in Waldshut/Dogern in the Upper Rhine region of Germany. With eight European subsidiaries of which four are manufacturing units and more than 30 agencies around the world, the company employs 682 members of staff.

The company sees its strengths in the balanced combination of innovative product design, high quality, application of durable designs and materials, a sense of ecological responsibility, and the ergonomic features of the products. Evidence of the high standards of quality is provided not only by the many awards but also by certification to ISO 14001, and by being the first company in the entire German furniture sector to participate in the EU standard eco-audit. Sedus supplies a wide variety of products for all kinds of applications. The range for administration areas, conferences and relaxation includes millions of technical and visual variations.

The accent is on functionality and a high level of utility with the family of office chairs for the back office, and a masterly mix of materials and visible technology in the front office; always with the intention of simultaneously achieving ideal ergonomic design and exquisite appearance. The matching range of visitors' chairs and conference chairs is a natural part of this, as are the mobile, flexible table systems for multifunctional room use.

Sedus Turn Around designed by Udo Hasenbein. A new seating concept can be astonishingly simple: the backrest of "turn around" rotates through 360 degrees, while the seat and base remain stationary. Designer Udo Hasenbein has created a new freedom for sitting at meetings and in day rooms or reception areas. "Turn Around" encourages flexible sitting positions, and this unusual chair asks to be handled playfully. The fresh colours of the plastic, leather or fabric upholstery and the non-wearing mechanical parts both add to its appeal.

Design awards 2002: iF Product Design Award for the Sedus corner lounge/conference chair, Industrie Forum Design (Germany)

Design awards 2001: iF Product Design Awards for the Sedus open up swivel chair, Sedus turn around swivel chair and Sedus time out MS folding table, Industrie Forum Design (Germany) / red dot for the Sedus open up swivel chair, Sedus turn around swivel chair, Sedus time out MS folding table and Sedus time out MS multipurpose chair, Design Zentrum Nordrhein Westfalen (Germany) / NeoCon Silver Award (USA) for the Sedus open up swivel chair / German Prize for Business Communication / Good Design Award (USA) for the Sedus turn around swivel chair / Good Design Award (USA) for the Sedus open up work assistant

Sedus Open up designed by Mathias Seiler Sedus incorporated the findings of specialists in occupational medicine and sleep researchers in the design of a new product. "open up", an office chair for sitting and lying, allows a quick nap, just as it permits working in a relaxed posture. The backrest with the new "Similar" mechanism provides a large reclining angle of about 45 degrees. The adjustable headrest supports the head and neck even when they are tilted forward to look at a monitor screen. The "ottoman", a leg support on castors or glides, completes the lying posture. A notebook computer can be operated on the adjustable "work assistant". A gas lift mechanism allows quick and easy adjustment to any height. Fully extended, the "work assistant" becomes a lectern.

Germany

Siemens-Electrogeräte
GmbH

Hochstrasse 17
81669 München
Tel. +49 89 45 90 - 09
Fax +49 89 45 90 - 23 47
www.siemens.com

Siemens

As an inventor and entrepreneur of vision in the second half of the 19th century, Werner von Siemens (1816-1892) contributed substantially not only to the new discipline of electrical engineering, but also to the development of the electrical industry. With the construction of his pointer telegraph he laid the foundation for the "Telegraphen-Bauanstalt von Siemens & Halske", the Siemens & Halske Telegraph Construction Company, which rapidly became an international business.

Through the successful completion of highly complex technological projects involving considerable financial risk, such as the construction of the Indo-European telegraph line from London to Calcutta or the laying of large transatlantic cables, the company soon became known all over the world.

In 1866 Werner von Siemens made what was probably his most important contribution to electrical engineering with his discovery of the dynamoelectric principle, thus paving the way for the use of electricity as a source of energy. Ever since its foundation in 1847, Siemens has addressed the challenge of shaping the future with innovations.
Today, Siemens AG with its head offices in Berlin and Munich is a world leader in electronics and electrical engineering. Over 450,000 staff develop and manufacture products, plan and construct plant and systems, and provide customised services. In over 190 countries, the company founded more than 150 years ago supports its customers with innovative technologies and extensive know-how in finding solutions to their commercial and technical problems. The company is active in the fields of information and communications, automation and control, power, transportation, medical technology and lighting.

Thanks to its highly innovative and reliable products, Siemens Electrogeräte is a pacesetter in the household appliance industry. The company will continue expanding business on this basis, with a focus on Internet-ready appliances for the smart house of the future. Many of the products have electronic controls which facilitate a greater array of features while substantially cutting operating costs. The development of advanced communications technologies is a further focus of the company's activities. Its e-commerce platform is enabling the company to accelerate and optimise communication processes with its commercial partners in Europe.

F.A. Porsche has designed a series of electrical goods that are functional and incorporate innovative technology. 2.2 mm polished metal ensures the required degree of robustness and durability at thermally important points.

Design Awards: Siemens has won the iF Product Design Award from Industrie Forum Hannover (Germany) about 30 times in the past five years, and also the international "red dot award" from the Design Zentrum Nordrhein Westfalen in Essen (Germany) about 30 times. In 1995 the company was honoured with the award for the Design Team of the Year by the Design Zentrum Nordrhein Westfalen. These awards have clearly demonstrated that Siemens is one of the leading industrial design companies. A company spokesman comments: "Good design defines and consolidates the brand image and has come to symbolise personal lifestyle. However, good design involves more than a beautiful exterior. Instead, it takes its orientation from handling, from touching and operating. It makes the product usable and comprehensible. At Siemens, design is intended to convey experiences providing feedback, resulting in simplified operation. To the user, it aims to convey the benefits of the technology, translating innovations into personal experiences that make sense."

Japan

Sony

Sony Corporation Tokyo

6-7-35 Kitashinagawa
Shinagawa-ku
Tokyo 141-0001 Japan
Tel. +81 3 54 48-21 11
Fax +81 3 54 48-22 44
www.sony.net

"Doing what has never been done before." Masaru Ibuka / Founder and Chief Advisor – The Sony spirit is all about bravely setting out to do what has never been done before.

"Markets are created, not conformed to." Akio Morita / Founder and Honorary Chairman – If you survey the public for what they think they need, you'll always be behind in this world. You'll never catch up unless you think one to ten years in advance and create a market for the items you think the public will accept at that time.

"Developing products that pull at the heartstrings." Norio Ohga / Chairman of the Board – The bottom line is that the product itself must be good. It is important to develop products that will make the customers think, "I'm glad I bought it", "I'm glad I used it", "I'm glad I had it".

"Digital Dream Kids" Nobuyuki Idei / Chairman and CEO – The slogan "Digital Dream Kids" expresses what we do at Sony. With a child's sense of wonder, we work to make new creations.

"Designing products that have a philosophy" Kunitake Ando / President and COO – All original products are based on a philosophy. The role for us is to communicate that philosophy to our customers.

Sony's corporate philosophy is at the heart of its design: Since its founding in 1946, the Company's innovation has yielded many revolutionary new products and a very strong brand. It's a brand built on the essentials – high quality and reliability in every product. But there's another key contributor to the outstanding image the company enjoys – Sony design.
Since the very beginning, the Sony Corporation has been characterised by the passion to "do what has never been done before," by the drive to "always stay one step ahead."

TR-610 Transistor Radio, 1958

This intrepid corporate spirit has clearly shaped the mission of Sony design: "To create high-performance products that are beautiful and easy to use, with a distinctive Sony flair." This is the philosophy - indeed the rule - behind the long line of uniquely attractive Sony designs.

Sony Design – The sculptor behind the company's countless hit products: Since its founding, Sony has sought to create products that stand out clearly in the market, which explains the company's consistent attention to design. In the late 1950s – before the field of industrial design even had its beginnings in Japan - Sony launched a product design programme, scouring the nation to bring designers in-house. As recognition of the Sony name grew, ambitious young designers beat a path to Sony's door, attracted by

TV8-301 Transistor Television, 1960

TFM-110 Transistor Radio, 1965

the company's enthusiasm for design. In those days, product planners, engineers, designers – even top executives – all worked together to improve product designs. Out of this intense early collaboration came the now typical Sony zeal for innovation. As the designers used to say, "Put brains with technical expertise, and you'll do what has never been done before." To this day, these words express the philosophy of Sony design. And this spirit is alive and kicking in the hearts of all the company's designers.

The following four essential design terms set the tone for the things we do:

Originality – At the heart of Sony design objectives: The Sony design community continues to strive to create boldly original ideas in this age of digital technology. For Sony, digital products are all about the people who use them. It only stands to reason that these products should be designed with a human touch. Putting people at the heart of design is the key to Sony's distinctive creativity.

Form follows function – Design that starts from the product concept: Just after the Sony design community was established in 1961, the company introduced its black and silver design theme, giving the Sony image an enormous lift. The idea was to do away with excessive ornamentation and to accentuate a powerful, high performance, professional impression through the use of simple, cool colors.

WM-2 "Walkman"
Portable Stereo Cassette Player, 1981

SCPH-1000
PlayStation, 1994

DVW-700WS
Digital BETACAM, 1994

Enhancing lifestyles: Creating products that strike a universal chord in people everywhere: People often say that the Sony Walkman changed their lives. But in fact, the Walkman's success has to be credited to people's desire to add "music-on-the-go" to their lives. The Walkman touched the hearts of consumers by enabling listeners to go mobile with their favourite musical environment, to add their own personal sound to any scene at any time. The story of the Walkman is a perfect illustration of what it takes to change consumer lifestyles – a product that strikes a universal chord, touching hearts everywhere it goes.

Ease of operation: On-site with users, watching and listening to understand their needs: Sony design is typified by the company's approach to creating devices for professional users. The company treasures the voice of the professional equipment operator. Take the example of Sony professional video cameras. From the shape of each button and dial to the position of every switch, these sophisticated devices deliver optimum functionality while also giving full expression to the beauty of function itself. Sony listens carefully to camera operators and observes the conditions in which equipment is used. The company's designers see themselves as manufacturing professionals committed to continuous product improvement, and collaborate with users of professional equipment on improving designs.

Sony Design Centre
As the new millennium begins to take shape, the Sony Design Centre has reinvented itself to take advantage of new technologies and make the most of today's rapidly changing markets.

In addition to the design team in Japan, the Sony Design Centre has offices located worldwide – in Europe, Singapore, and the United States. By reflecting regional preferences and values in Sony designs, the Design Centre strives not only to add value to current businesses and create new possibilities, but also to generate a much more exciting design and operational environment.

The Design behind the Dream
Whether at the birth of a new technology or when struggling in the intense competition of a matured market, the prime directive for the Sony designer is to dream - to offer new technologies, lifestyles and enjoyments to consumers through Sony products, services, and interactive and graphic design.

Sony Design will continue to communicate the unique Sony identity, inspiring consumers with a constant stream of innovative products and services. This is the key to the strength of the Sony brand. By constantly "betraying" consumer expectations – always to their benefit – Sony Design brings the world the distinct pleasure of continuous astonishment and delight.

DSC-F1 Cyber-shot
Digital Still Camera, 1997

PCG-505 VAIO
Personal Computer, 1997

SDR-4X
Biped Entertainment Robot, 2002

Pride in European design

Adding the values of extreme usability and advanced engineering and technology to contemporary European design – with the lifestyles it suggests and its sophisticated appreciation of texture, high-quality finish and form - has been the central mission of Sony's European design. The recurring theme has been the pure geometric form, shapes that complement a flat display, yielding a sheer simplicity with functional design value. The values created for the first-generation Art Couture models remain timeless, conveying a romantic yet impartial image that is simple, luxurious and modern.

A universal product like the television will always have cultural barriers to surmount. The local touch of the designers enables Sony to achieve a level of expression that speaks the right language for each location. Sony products have crossed every border to become truly European.

Six design criteria were followed to achieve a prominent, technologically advanced, stylish element of furniture.

Real materials: Use familiar materials that are common in furniture, but not seen in consumer electronic goods, such as aluminum, steel and glass

Quality and value: Exploit the optimum suitability of the materials and the appreciation of surface finish.

Hidden technology: Technology on demand, but passive when not required.

Sophisticated detailing: Continuity of form language throughout, and an interplay between crisp, hard edges and soft, flowing surfaces.

Furniture integration: Integration with contemporary furniture, a seamless style with its stand.

European interior setting: Consideration of atmosphere and interior decor.

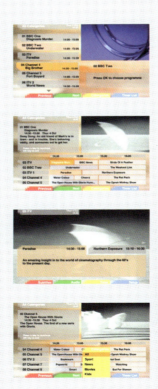

Sony Digital TV: Visual references to the "digital" semantic give this product its distinctive character. Compared to analog products, the digital product offers greater scope for the introduction of new creative languages and visual metaphors. The design features strongly stylised details, conveying the "network connection" concept, and the "physical" layers of the product reflect functionality in their form. Using a series of hierarchical layers, which help shape the meaning of the visual and interactive experience, a single seamless design language stretches through both hardware and software.

One of the major aims of the designers was to create a "portal" image. New technologies serve as a "window" for delivery of the digital experience - all with a simple "formal" and spatial treatment. This is a key design statement differentiating the digital from the analog - the first layer. The interface is the second layer, the venue for interaction and product functionality. This is followed in order by the other semantic elements, such as the "intelligent central nervous system" working as a data processor, finally ending with the "gateway" for the flow of information. The metaphorical biological concept is brought to fruition by suiting up the product in a sensual skin.

Human interface design for the Sony NX100 began with an effort to develop a non-PC-style GUI. While the digital TV is a highly computerised product, users, by contrast, are looking for a comfortable face in their TV set, not a computerized, high-tech character. The designers refused to use 3D graphics, so often employed with typical multimedia products. Instead, they built the GUI as a collection of 2D graphic pieces montaged on semi-transparent layers. A new concept was born: "Not 3D Effects, but a Feel of Depth." By using semi-transparent layers, the NX100's GUI has achieved a subtle feel of comfortable depth, implying an entrance to the digital network world.

Poland

Studio Idea

Studio IDEA Ltd

Pl.Wilsona 4 m.54
01-627, Warszawa
Tel. +48 22 832 3391
Fax +48 22 832 3392
Mobile: +48 602 178589
www.ideadesign.com.pl
studio@ideadesign.com.pl

Studio IDEA is a leading design company in Poland, and its professional activities include three basic divisions dedicated to graphic and editorial design (2D), industrial design (3D), and new media (multi D).

A creative team of experienced designers and engineers supported by group of assistants and technicians is ready to solve even the most complex problems encountered by clients. The industrial design department (3D) is perfectly equipped for design and engineering services based on CAD/ CAM/ CAE solutions by Unigraphics (3 workplaces), I-DEAS (2 workplaces), ProEngineer (3 workplaces) and other leading software packages.

The samples of Studio IDEA design works presented show high tech laboratory equipment, a portable cash register and a single user golf car for handicapped persons, all of them designed for internationally operating companies.

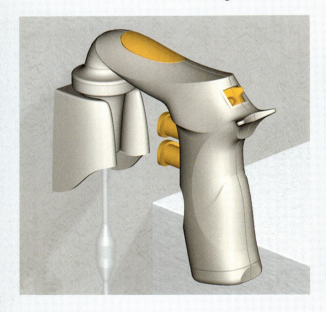

High precision pipetting device designed for HTL S.A., distributed on the international market.

Single user golf car specifically designed for handicapped persons playing golf while unable to walk, offered for the American market.

Portable cash register designed for Central European emerging markets.

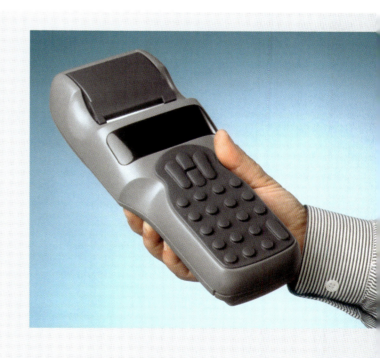

India

TATA

**TATA Engineering
and Locomotive Co. Ltd.**

Bombay House
24, Homi Mody Street
Hutatma Chowk,
Mumbai 400 001
Tel. +91 22 56 65 82 82
Fax +91 22 22 04 54 74
vs@telco.co.in
www.telcoindia.com

Tata Engineering and Locomotive Co. Ltd. was established in 1945 to manufacture locomotives – to help provide the wheels for a nation that needed development. It started producing commercial vehicles in 1954 and today ranks as one of the world's largest commercial vehicle manufacturers. It is India's largest exporter of automobiles today, and its products can be seen in Europe, Africa, Asia and Australia.

In 1999, the company made its foray into the passenger car market with the Indica, a tribute to the company's design, engineering and manufacturing capabilities. Building on the contemporary technology of the Indica, Tata Engineering launched India's indigenous sedan, christened the Indigo. The word is reflective of the sentiment that India is all set to 'Go' and join the ranks of leading global automobile makers. Today, with India's largest range of commercial, passenger and multi-utility vehicles available in petrol, diesel and CNG models, Tata Engineering is the only fully integrated Indian automobile company. It has subsidiaries that specialise in technology solutions, manufacture of machine tools and factory automation equipment, axles, transmissions and construction equipment, and international collaborations with leading design and styling houses. Tata Engineering also has its own in-house Engineering Research Centre with scientists and engineers working round the clock to innovate and bring the best to the fore.

"One must forever strive for excellence, or even perfection, in any task, however small, and never be satisfied with second best" – the late J.R.D. Tata. Chairman, Tata Group (1938-1991). The Tata group follows this credo in all its systems and processes. The Tata name has survived for 130 years with a commitment to improving the quality of life by continually pursuing excellence. The trusted Tata mark is a part of everyday life for any Indian, right from something as ubiquitous as salt to something as distinctive as India's top selling compact passenger car – the Indica. The Tata name has gained recognition for leadership with trust. There have been a number of pioneering efforts in the group's long and historic association with India, like the first private sector steel mill, the first private sector power utility, the first luxury hotel chain, the first international airline and the first software venture, to cite a few examples.

Tata Engineering adopts a proactive approach in reducing environmental hazards and rendering its services while maintaining an ecological balance. Today its utility vehicles and passenger cars are capable of meeting the most stringent European standards. Tata Engineering received the Central Pollution Control Board Award for Environment Protection for its innovative and consistent efforts in endeavouring to restore the ecological balance.

Tata Engineering's vision to deliver the best and ensure customer satisfaction has earned it a dominant position in the Indian automobile industry.

The Indica: Tata Engineering embarked on a bold course to design, develop and manufacture a contemporary small car with state-of-the-art technology, and entered the globally competitive market. It was no mean task set before the design team. The car needed to have exceptional interior space with compact exterior dimensions and class leading fuel economy coupled with world class safety standards. The design had to convey a contemporary, sporty and cheerful personality, and all that at an affordable cost. These are the makings of the Indica. A car that was rolled out in 33 months from the concept stage.

For this significant contribution to the Indian automobile industry, Tata Engineering was awarded the National Award for R&D Efforts by the Indian Ministry of Science and Technology. The car was launched amid great euphoria in the country. True to expectations, it is now India's top selling passenger car in the competitive compact car segment amongst a host of models from 14 global auto makers.

The Indica will, no doubt, be one of many cars from the Tata Engineering stable to adorn and carry forth the symbol of creative talent and design competence of Tata Engineering.

Japan

Toyota

Toyota Motor Corporation

1 Toyota-Cho,
Aichi Prefecture
471-8571 Japan
Tel. +81 565 28 21 21
www.toyota.co.jp

The Toyota Motor Co. Ltd. was first established in 1937 as a spin-off from Toyoda Automatic Loom Works, one of the world's leading manufacturers of weaving machinery. The Toyoda Automatic Loom Works was then headed by Japan's "King of Inventors" Sakichi Toyoda.

Toyota launched its first small car (SA Model) in 1947. Production systems were improved in the late 1950s, culminating in the establishment of the 'Toyota Production System. This became known as TPS in 1970, but was actually established much earlier by Taiichi Ohno. Based on the principles of Jidoka, Just-in-time and Kaizen, the system is a major factor in the reduction of inventories and defects in the plants of Toyota and its suppliers, and it underpins all their operations across the World. August 1997 marked the 60th anniversary of TMC. Today, Toyota is the world's third largest manufacturer of automobiles in unit sales and in net sales. It is by far the largest Japanese automotive manufacturer, from minivehicles to large trucks producing more than 5.5 million vehicles per year, equivalent to one every six seconds. It is nearly 30 years since Toyota founded its first overseas design studio, Calty Design, in Los Angeles. Now, together with Calty, ED2 in Nice, Tokyo Design Center, and Head Office Design Center, a 4 point satellite system has been created, further enhancing the level of Toyota Design. Toyota has always regarded its satellite offices not just as groups of local designers designing for local markets, but as a unique culturally mixed network where different ways of thinking are used to stimulate new ideas.

The Prius: Production Car 2000, designed by Head Office Design Center. Since the first car, "Type AA" was unveiled in 1936, the passion for innovation of the founder Kiichiro Toyoda has passed from generation to generation of Toyota engineers and designers. "Prius", the world's first mass-produced hybrid car, is one example of that spirit. Ever since its debut in 1997, the Prius, with its groundbreaking Toyota Hybrid System (THS) and advanced design and packaging, has been hailed as a next-generation four-door sedan for the 21st century.

Yaris: Production Car 1999, designed by ED2. In the case of the Yaris, ideas from European designers were used to stimulate ideas from designers in the USA and Japan to enhance the final product. Because of this approach the product has a universal appeal. Toyota thinks the co-existence of different values is the fundamental base of the company's culture.

In order to meet the needs of the global 21st century, Toyota believes that a symbiotic design culture is a necessity. Yaris won a Special Prize in The World's Most Beautiful Automobile Award 1999, for its unconventional styling. It was the first Toyota model to have been designed in Europe, and has met with great success. The Yaris is an innovative design that re-defines the meaning of the mainstream compact car.

The design concept has achieved a clear aim – that the Yaris is enjoyable and vibrant whilst at the same time incorporates the big cabin packaging so necessary to its function.

Urban Utility Vehicle UUV Show Car in Geneva Motor Show 2002, designed by ED2. The Toyota UUV is a new generation of multi cross-over vehicle which blends the best characteristics of SUVs with premium car design, road behaviour, comfort and performance. The UUV concept blends hatchback, sedan and wagon into one harmonised multi-cross body. A key feature of the interior is the full width, dash mounted screen which offers entertainment and navigational functions to both driver and passenger. The system is called 'Glass Vision'.

Personalization On Demand p.o.d. Show Car in Tokyo Motor Show 2001, designed by Head office Design Center. The p.o.d was developed in conjunction with Sony Corporation. The p.o.d has four individual seats designed to allow passengers to communicate together. It recognises that modern technology enables the car-user relationship to develop as both man and the machine learn more about each other.

Dual Mode Traveler DMT Show Car in Tokyo Motor Show 2001, designed by Tokyo Design Center. The DMT is a special-purpose 'cruiser style' vehicle with a 'drive mode' and 'stay mode' which provides versatile functions to support the pursuit of personal interests in a mobile, individualistic lifestyle. The DMT's interior is designed with many configurations to adapt easily to a variety of activities, according to its users' interests. Third party equipment can be installed to widen the available options.

Lexus: Since the launch of the LS400 in 1989, Lexus has worked to create vehicles of refinement and style. The Lexus aim has always been to create a new definition of luxury, not simply ostentatious, but a more refined, pure version of luxury. Lexus design could be described as intriguing simplicity that has been derived from the seamless anticipation of the customers' needs and desires.

Lexus IS 300: Production Car 2000, designed by Head Office Design Center. The IS 300 is a compelling challenge to European sport sedans, packaging a high-performance powertrain, rear-drive chassis layout, and a sportscar-inspired interior in a taut, wedged-shape body. It received The World's Most Beautiful Automobile Award in the Middle-class saloon category.

Lexus SC 430: Production Car 2001, designed by ED2. The Lexus SC series was introduced into the Lexus brand in 1991. The latest model, SC 430, was designed from the outset to be an all-round luxury cabriolet, with an integrated all-metal retractable roof offering the best of both worlds, combining open-air driving pleasure with Lexus standards of comfort and refinement.

Bob Daenen
Vice President, Innovation

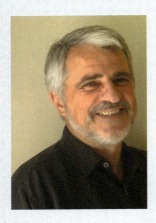

USA

Tupperware Corporation

P.O. Box 2353
Orlando, FL 32802

Tupperware General
Services N. V.
Tupperware Europe, Africa
& Middle East
Design Department
Pierre Corneliskaai 35
B-9300 Aalst
Tel. 0032 53 72 75 41
Fax 0032 53 72 75 40
bobdaenen@tupperware.com
www.tupperware.com

Tupperware

Tupperware's origins go back to 1944, when Earl S. Tupper, a chemist and the first person to use polyethylene in the household sector, founded the "Tupper Plastic Company". One of the first products, the "Wonderbowl", was launched on the market in 1946. At the start, the Tupperware products were sold in department stores, hardware shops and other retail outlets, but it soon became apparent that the retailers were not sufficiently informed to explain the air and watertight safety seal effectively.

In response, the home demonstration system for Tupperware products was developed, allowing them to be presented in detail to the customers right where they would be used – in the home. The system proved so successful that retail distribution was eventually stopped. Since 1951, Tupperware has been exclusively demonstrated and marketed through the company's own organisation. Earl S. Tupper has long found a place in our vocabulary with terms like "Tupper party", and the airtight plastic containers have been an integral part of our everyday culture for over 50 years.

Today, Tupperware Corporation is a multinational company, and one of the world's leading direct sellers. Through its Tupperware brand, the company provides consumers with food storage, preparation and serving items as well as business opportunities, in more than 100 countries. In short, Tupperware is everywhere and Tupperware products have a high globalisation quality, as a result of which they can be found in most households in the world. With their uncompromising usefulness, the products overcome the obstacles of everyday life and leave nothing to be desired even when used ad hoc as problem solvers.

Fridge Smart Range, 2000: The ACE (Atmosphere Controlled Environment) container system has been developed on the basis of the latest scientific findings to enable fruit and vegetables to be kept longer. The form of the containers reflects natural laws. They have a corrugated bottom that works like an integrated freshness`grating with the food resting on the peaks of the corrugations. The white vent buttons, which are used to optimise the atmosphere inside the containers, are similarly corrugated. The grained outside surface reinforces the visual impression of the corrugations.

Design Awards: Tupperware products are part of the Design Collection of numerous museums around the world and Tupperware received 42 design awards from different institutions in the past five years:

Award for excellent design from Industrie Forum Hannover (Germany) / Red Dot for High and the Highest Design Quality from Design Zentrum Nordrhein Westfalen in Essen (Germany) / Good Design Award from The Chicago Athenaeum Museum of Architecture & Design (USA) / Janus Award from French Institute of Design in Paris (France) / Best Product 1999 from Vizo Organisation in Brussels (Belgium) / Silver Award 2000 from Industrial Designers' Society of America / Corporate Achievement Award 2001, Smithsonian's Cooper-Hewitt National Design Museum (USA).

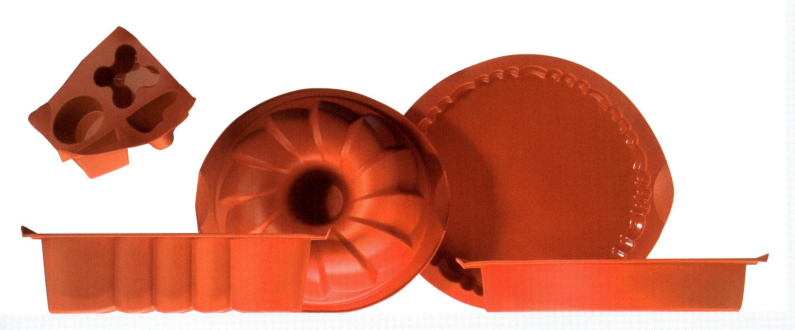

Silicone Moulds, 2001: These silicone moulds are suitable for freezer, fridge, oven or microwave. They are temperature resistant from -25°C to +220°C. The special silicone material is unbreakable and flexible. Its non-stick properties mean that deep frozen or baked food slips out of the mould easily. The series comprises five different motifs, the rectangular Prince model, the round Princess and Queen models and a larger round mould named Crown. All the moulds can be washed in hot soapy water and are dishwasher safe.

Chef Series Forged Knife Collection: The Chef Series knife set, a collection of nine hand polished professional grade forged Japanese stainless steel knives, represents an integration of four elements: design, material, performance and the fine art of hand craftsmanship. These knives, designed exclusively by Tupperware were created with intensive input from chefs in Europe and the USA. The Chef Series forged knives collection departs from the traditional cliché of heavy, masculine, tool-like chef's knives elevating the classic image of kitchen product to a new level of design elegance.

Prof. Yrjö Wiherheimo
chief designer
and artistic director

Finland

Vivero Oy

Hämeentie 11
00530 Helsinki
Tel. +358 9 774-53 3-0
Fax +358 9 774-53 311
www.vivero.fi

Vivero

The Vivero Oy furniture company was established in 1980, when four idealists - Yrjö Wiherheimo, Veli-Pekka Vasama, Risto Lappalainen and Matti Uusitalo - pooled their resources. Timo Vesara became the first managing director. The name of the company carries oblique references to the names of the founders, but it also brings to mind vivacity and the colour green. Wiherheimo no longer wanted to draw for his own pleasure and for the odd client, but craved to see his designs in production instead. The new company had only existed for a month or so and its product range consisted of two chairs, when the entrepreneurs had to make a decision on participation in the Copenhagen furniture fair. Vivero's pace was way too brisk for the association of Finnish furniture exporters, who refused to include them on their stand. This turned out to be a stroke of luck, as Wiherheimo and Vesara applied for an export subsidy and put up their own show in a 19 m² space in the Bella Center's hall K, managing to spread the word so efficiently that as early as in June 1980 design guru Alessandro Mendini was in Finland to check out Visio and Verde, Vivero's two chairs. In July Mendini's article was published in the design bible Domus, and the following autumn saw a complete success for Vivero at the Milan furniture fair.

Soft-2 Design Kai Korhonen, 2000

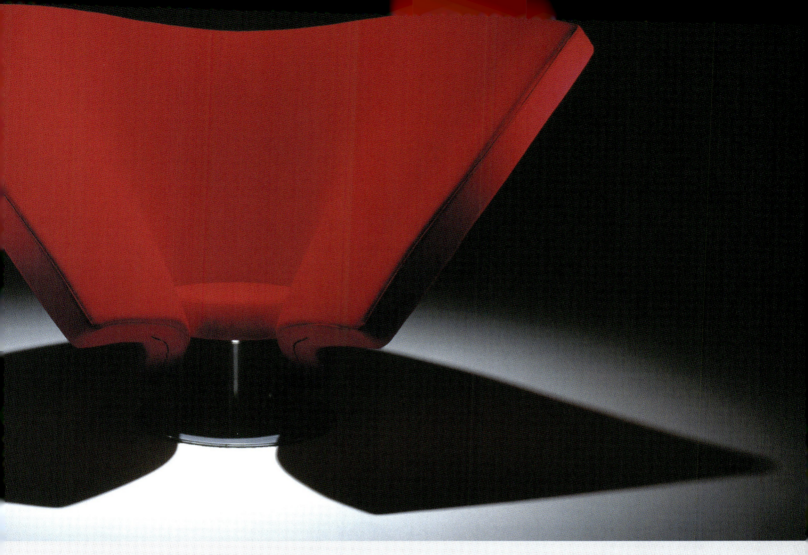

In August 1981 the International Council of Societies of Industrial Design (ICSID) arranged a conference in Helsinki. Vivero mounted a contemporary exhibition at the Helsinki City Art Museum, illustrating the making of a chair detail by detail and presenting the company's component philosophy. Numerous other design exhibitions were also arranged around Helsinki during the conference: Finland had made a come-back in design.

Furniture production - design and manufacture - is simultaneously both a part of material culture production and a distinctly separate way of thinking and doing. It is a special case of material culture production, which is best understood by demonstrating what constitutes the field of production and how it is divided in two, so that the parts dominated by the artistic interest on the one hand and economic interest on the other are sometimes placed in opposition. From the point of view of industrial art, a piece of furniture is a special physical commodity, because its symbolic value is exceptionally high. There is a heated debate in the field of furniture production about what is important and worth striving for. That is, which of the possible properties and aspects of a piece of furniture is the most valuable.

The antithesis and debate of the artistic and economic interest of industrial art can be understood as follows. While the economic interest of furniture production emphasises economic profitability (volume, sales figures, turnover and profit), the artistically orientated side places great value on the aesthetic quality of production, which, by definition, is difficult to demonstrate or measure.

The basis for all commercial activity, "business is business", in its extreme form, means that it is worthwhile making anything that is economically profitable. In the artistically-oriented side of production, the extreme case of which is "l'art pour l'art", the fact that a product should do well according to the internal criteria of industrial art is, by far, more important than how well or badly it sells. The important thing is that the object represents good design and it does well in the debate on the design of objects. In the artistically-dominated side of industrial art, the value of an object cannot be reduced to mere commercial success. Instead, the success of an object is measured by the independent evaluation criteria of industrial art, for instance, how the object is received in exhibitions of industrial art, museums, collections, publications, magazines, books or school curricula.

Criticism which is not directly linked to the commercial interest and success cannot be bought and is particularly difficult to achieve. This kind of disinterested criticism and prestige can be bestowed only by those who simultaneously are the closest colleagues and fiercest rivals, for instance, another designer and manufacturer, who well knows the independent evaluation criteria of industrial art. Various public demonstrations of respect, such as awards, exhibitions, publications, collections and museums are visible signs of the independent status of industrial art.

Modern furniture design operates on a market which is only emerging, a market it has, as it were, to create. It does not answer a ready, existing demand, content with only satisfying those needs, but creates its own demand by simultaneously creating new objects and their users. Modern furniture design creates new types of objects and new ways of seeing, experiencing and using them. This naturally is an expensive long-term activity, requiring time and effort, in which markets and profits can be far off in the future.

Industrial art can be seen as a world view, a special way of looking at and seeing the world. It differs from the usual ways of seeing the world in that it pays particular attention to the aesthetic and functional quality of products and gives them priority over other properties of the object, as properties worth extra effort and struggle and debate with other industrial art producers.

Where others only see ordinary technical, material and economic objects, industrial art producers, scholars, designers, manufacturers, retailers, and consumers see extraordinary cult objects, which are extraordinary just because seeing them requires time and effort and is difficult. This way of seeing and distinguishing objects, according to their aesthetic and functional properties, is not a God-given talent but the result of long practice and training. It means continually thinking thoughts and performing actions, so that they become "second nature", an internalised, natural and unforced way of thinking, believing, feeling, seeing and acting, which cannot be exchanged for another, and which usually cannot and need not be explained.

Vivero markets not only goods and functional solutions, but also images and knowledge on the impact of design at large. The sales staff consists of people who know how to relate to architects, designers and buyers alike. Many new and traditional companies find that Vivero's concept matches their corporate image, and the clientele also includes various cultural institutions, universities and IT companies. Vivero has become an integral part of contemporary architecture, its designs enhancing and accompanying spatial design. Today, the twenty-year-old Vivero is an original, recognisable concept in design.

Visio-100/k Design Yrjö Wiherheimo & Simo Heikkilä, 1980

Plus-Z Design Yrjö Wiherheimo & Pekka Kojo, 1999

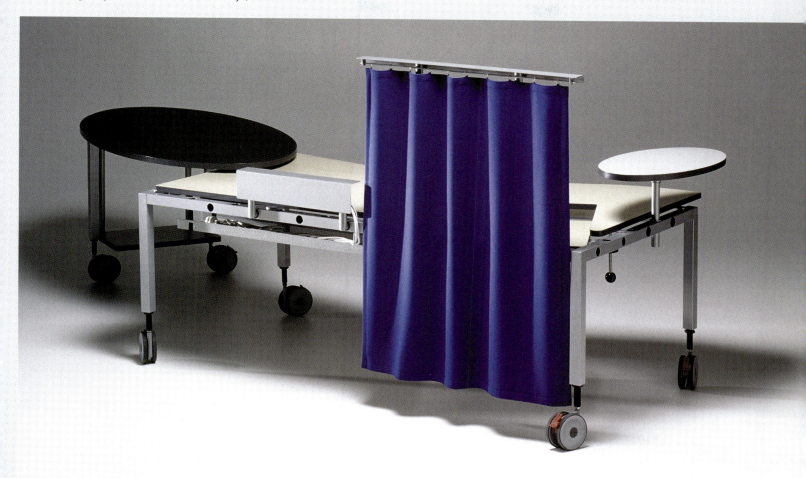

Prizes and Design Awards: Ornamo Pallo Award 2001, The Finnish Association of Designers Ornamo, Helsinki (Finland) / Ilmari Tapiovaara Prize 2001 awarded to Yrjö Wiherheimo, University of Art and Design Helsinki (Finland) / "Habitare Top Ten" Prize 1999, Finnish Fair Corporation, Helsinki (Finland) / MD's "10 Office Systems" selection 1995, Stuttgart (Germany) / "Habitare Top Ten" Prize 1995, Finnish Fair Corporation, Helsinki (Finland) / National nomination for Scandinavian Design Management Prize 1994 / S.I.O. Prize, The Best Finnish Interior Design Project 1991, Finnish Association of Interior Architects, Helsinki (Finland) / Lahti Fair Furniture Diploma 1986, Lahti (Finland) / S.I.O. Prize, the Best Finnish Furniture Design 1984, Finnish Association of Interior Architects, Helsinki (Finland) / Habitare Prize 1981, Finnish Fair Corporation, Helsinki (Finland)

Designs at permanent collections of the following museums: Victoria and Albert Museum, London / Cooper-Hewitt Museum, New York / Kunstgewerbe Museum, Hamburg / Kunstindustrimuseet i Oslo, Oslo / Museum of Applied Arts, Helsinki / Kunstindustrimuseet, København / Athenaeum, Chicago

Designers: Yrjö Wiherheimo, Pekka Kojo, Kai Korhonen, Timo Ripatti, Kaare Falbe, Lars Larsen / Corporate Identity & Graphic Design: Aimo Katajamäki

Germany

Vorwerk

Vorwerk & Co. KG

Mühlenweg 17-37
42270 Wuppertal
Tel. +49 202 56 40
Fax +49 202 56 43 271
corporate.communication@vorwerk.de
www.vorwerk.de

What should one do when the quality aspects of a product are concealed? Customers have to be made aware of them. And for this reason direct selling was born. For more than 70 years now the Vorwerk company, located in Wuppertal (Germany), has been manufacturing high-quality vacuum cleaners that are sold to customers by a team of self-employed sales advisers. The homecare products are demonstrated in the home of the prospective customer – i.e. at that place where the appliances will be used in the future – and they show what they can do: deep cleaning of carpets, carpeting and hard floors in an environmentally-friendly fashion.

As opposed to the retail business where quite often price is the only factor which assists customers in making a decision, the Vorwerk Kobold can demonstrate all its qualities in the household and show its strengths in comparison to competitors. Vorwerk has been most successful in Germany and many other countries with its concept of developing, manufacturing and directly selling high-quality household appliances. Over 80 million Kobolds alone – with their electrically-driven accessory appliances (carpet brush, carpet freshener, Pulilux hard-floor cleaner and Polsterboy) – have left the company's manufacturing facilities to date. Business with the Kobold and its "sister", the extremely versatile kitchen appliance Thermomix, has long since overtaken the traditional carpeting business at Vorwerk, both in terms of turnover and profit, and has become the core business of the Vorwerk Group.

The Vorwerk Group, a family-owned company since 1883 that is managed by the great-grandson of the founder at the head of a four-strong executive board, today has some 45,000 staff. The Vorwerk direct sales world includes the Kobold Systems and Thermomix divisions for the manufacture and sale of Vorwerk products. In 2001 a new addition was made with the Lux Asia-Pacific division responsible for the sale of household appliances in the Far East. Since January 2002 Vorwerk has been on the market with the new Feelina ironing system and is currently establishing a direct sales organisation. In this way Vorwerk is constantly expanding its position as a leading direct-sales company operating world-wide. The design of the products, too, is aligned to the requirements of the direct sales system and is an important element of the cross-company corporate design concept. The development objectives are always to have the very highest functional and ergonomic quality combined with a surprising and innovative design. The long-term safeguarding of the brand design image of the product is of particular importance to the company.

Suction polisher Kobold PL 515: The Kobold PL 515 suction polisher, an appliance for the vacuuming, sweeping and polishing of hard floors, was launched in 2000. Sweeping and polishing functions are accomplished with three rotating pads. Vacuuming is effected mainly at the front tip and the rear section of the appliance.

Upright vacuum cleaner Vorwerk Kobold 131 with carpet brush Kobold EB 351: Launched in 1997, the Kobold 131 has a power input of maximum 700 W and a sophisticated filter system which also makes the appliance suitable for allergy sufferers. By avoiding technical shapes to a large extent, a light, novel and quite unique design appearance is achieved. The electrical carpet brush enhances dust and thread pick-up.

The Kobold System: The Kobold is a vacuum cleaner system which can be converted from an upright to a canister-type model. Besides the cleaning of carpeting with the EB 351 carpet brush and the cleaning of hard floors with the PL 515, the cleaning of furniture and upholstery is also possible with other accessories.

Japan

Yamaha

Yamaha Corporation

10-1 Nakazawa-cho
Hamamatsu City
Shizuoka Prefecture
Japan 430-8650
Tel. +81 53 460-28 83
Fax +81 53 463-49 22
www.global.yamaha.com

Founded in 1887, initially as an organ manufacturer, the Yamaha Corporation rapidly branched out into the production of pianos, harmonicas, and from the 1940s and 1950s also guitars and electronic organs. The now famous concert grand piano was launched in the 1960s, and the 1970s onwards saw diversification from the strict musical instrument field with the launch of an audio cassette deck designed by Mario Bellini in 1975, the DX7 digital synthesizer in 1983 and the WX7 wind MIDI controller in 1987. Yamaha's global network now spans subsidiaries and joint ventures in 20 countries in the Americas, Europe, Asia, and Australia, and it has manufacturing facilities in 15 locations in seven countries. The company employs 6394 people, 22 of whom are occupied in the Product Design Laboratory which was founded in 1963.

The products now comprise musical instruments, audio and telecommunications equipment, electronic devices, soundproofing and sports equipment.

A breakthrough in the musical instrument field was achieved in the 1990s with the launch of the silent instruments which have proven extremely popular and received numerous design awards, and the Millennium Disklavier Pro 2000 in the year 2000.
The company places sound, music and multimedia at the core of its existence, and its declared aim is "to contribute to the enhancement of the quality of life around the world". Its design philosophy revolves around the five key terms Integrity, Innovative, Aesthetic, Unobtrusive, and Social Responsibility.

Wind Controller, 1999

Design Awards 2001: red dot for SLB-100 Silent Upright Bass, Design Zentrum Nordrhein Westfalen (Germany) / SVC-200 Silent Cello, compact type Die Neue Sammlung, Permanent Collection (Germany)

Design Awards 2000: 46th Annual Design Review, Best of Category Consumer Products, The International Design Magazine (USA) / Industrial Design Excellence Award Bronze prize – Consumer Products (USA) / iF Design Award for WX5 Wind MIDI Controller, Excellent Design, Industrie Forum Design (Germany) / Red Dot for the Highest Design Quality for SVC-200 Silent Cello in the category Best of the Best, Design Zentrum Nordrhein Westfalen (Germany)

Design Awards 1999: 45th Annual Design Review, Design Distinction - Consumer Products, The International Design Magazine (USA) / iF Design Award for SV-100 Silent Violin, Most sought after Design, Industrie Forum Design (Germany) / Red Dot for High Design Quality for WX5 Wind MIDI Controller, Design Zentrum Nordrhein Westfalen (Germany)

Design Awards 1998: for WX5 Wind MIDI Controller Permanent Collection, The Chicago Athenaeum (USA) / 44th Annual Design Review - Design Distinction -Consumer Products, The International Design Magazine (USA) / Red Dot for the Highest Design Quality for SV-100 Silent Violin, Design Zentrum Nordrhein Westfalen (Germany)

Silent Cello, 2000

Israel

ZAG Industries

ZAG Industries Ltd.

Stanley Subsidiary
19 Ha'Melacha Street
New Industrial Zone
Rosh Ha'Ayin
48091
Tel. +972-3-90 20 200
Fax +972-3-90 20 222
support@zag.co.il
www.zag.co.il

Zvi Yemini founded ZAG® Industries in 1987, anticipating the growing need for advanced home and professional storage solutions. The challenge to innovate in a traditionally conservative market posed no obstacle. By 1993 ZAG was already developing, manufacturing and marketing unconventional plastic products incorporating combined materials such as metal, aluminium, wood and even fabric.

Realising that design and quality are the stepping stones to success, the ZAG Design Team, headed by Yehuda Einav, VP for Research and Development, has set numerous market trends. Functioning as a single entity is the ZAG philosophy, with the design, development and marketing teams working together towards a common goal: to address future market needs.

ZAG developments have tackled issues such as maximising limited work space, providing ease of use and assembly, and even developing tools for one handed operation. The ZAG team pays routine visits to customer sites gathering first hand information from contractors and end users. They continually seek new ways to pack functionality and design into a broad range of storage and DIY products - without compromising on cost-effectiveness.

By November 1996 ZAG had already secured a significant market share and proceeded to make an initial public offering on the NASDAQ stock exchange. It returned to private ownership in August 1998 when Stanley Works Inc. – recognising ZAG's potential – acquired 90.1% of its shares. Stanley Works Inc., founded 150 years ago, is a leading US based manufacturer of tools and doors.

Today, ZAG is a clear market leader. The product line spans home, storage, gardening and office use. ZAG solutions are available at almost every DIY retail chain worldwide. Products are divided into three major categories covering tool and accessory storage, worksite solutions such as workbenches and sawhorses, plus a wide variety of modular cabinets and shelves. Throughout its range of products, ZAG has been careful to develop state of the art storage solutions that conform to the most stringent international standards while maintaining a strict environment-friendly policy. ZAG continues to invest in R&D, harnessing advanced computer technology that has led to the development of numerous patented products. ZAG quickly evaluates new opportunities bringing innovative developments to market in the shortest possible time.

Design Awards: Selected for best DIY products and packaging at both the Chicago and Cologne hardware shows, ZAG was also twice the proud recipient of the prestigious "Good Design Award" for the years 2000 and 2001, awarded by the Chicago Athenaeum Museum of Architecture and Design. A range of ZAG products are also on display at other leading US museums including the Museum of Modern Art, New York.

The Mobile Project Centre: It is a multi-purpose rolling work station and tool storage unit. It features a comfortable 88cm/34.5 inch ergonomic work height with a 180kg/397 lbs load capacity, making it ideal for the toughest job. Each unit features fibreglass reinforced resin vice clamps, lockable heavy duty wheels for maximum stability, and an aluminium handle for easy and convenient transport.

The comprehensive Garage Workshop System from ZAG can transform any garage into a clean, tidy, and organised workspace. The system comprises cabinets and accessories, the workbench series and the mobile project centre. All units incorporate the unique ZAG combination of extra strength durable metal and high quality lightweight polypropylene. Snap assembled quickly and easily, all units come in knock down form and can easily be fitted into any size of car boot. Each cabinet has a 200kg/440 lbs load capacity and features fully extendable metal drawers with a 50kg/ 110 lbs capacity per drawer or shelf. The thick large wooden bench featured in the professional ZAG Workbench Series offers an extremely high load capacity of 700 kg/1,540 lbs, making it ideal for most heavy duty work. Robust and sturdy, the benches have a comfortable 90cm/35.5 inch ergonomic work height, featuring fully extendable metal drawers, a long metal shelf for extra heavy tools and pegboard sides to conveniently hang tools.

Adjustable Folding Sawhorse: The Adjustable Folding Sawhorse, a registered patent, is a multi-level workhorse that is easily adjusted to optimal height and width. It has an extremely high load capacity of 455kg/ 1,000 lbs per pair of workhorses, making it suitable for almost every heavy duty job. Features include saw v-groove attachments for aligning and securing pipes or lumber, which significantly facilitates cutting and sawing. This highly stable workhorse is made of polypropylene and features non-skid rubber coated soles. Recognised for its innovation and design, the Adjustable Folding Sawhorse was awarded the prestigious "Good Design Award" for the year 2000 by The Chicago Athenaeum: Museum of Architecture and Design (USA).

Folding Workbench: This versatile 3-in-1 combination unit is designed to serve as a workbench, vice or sawhorse. Its space-saving design and light weight enable it to be easily carried around and folded into a compact unit that fits into any size of car trunk. A large work surface can hold a heavy load capacity of 227 kg/500 lbs and includes several unique features including a moulded ruler for quick measurements, a built-in storage compartment for the vice clamps, a drill holder and a fastener's sorter. The ZAG Folding Workbench also features two patented heavy duty adjustable vice clamps that can accommodate almost anything from narrow pipes to wide planks, without marring the work piece. Engineered to offer a high level of stability on any job site, this multifunctional workbench features anti-slip rubber soles and is constructed of polypropylene for strength and durability.

Metal Rolling Workshop™: The concept from ZAG and the US based Group 500 designers is a modular professional workshop on wheels. It presents the ideal mobile storage and transportation solution for both oversized and small tools. Comprising three stand alone storage units that fit together as one, this durable yet lightweight workshop solution can be separated into three parts in seconds. The top unit comprises a toolbox featuring a stainless-steel diamond shaped top lid and a full- size removable tool tray, the drawer unit offers a large storage room, and the lower unit comprises a flip out metal bin for storage of extra large power tools such as a circular saw. Constructed from a combination of polypropylene and metal, it features two wide six inch rubber-coated wheels for maximum stability, and an adjustable telescopic aluminium handle for easy transport. Four integrated bungee cord holders on the sides are designed to carry other outsized accessories.

Tool Organizer The ZAG Tool Organizer provides a comprehensive storage solution for both small accessories and hand-held tools. Made of polypropylene, this robust storage utility offers a total of 39 different compartments. Divided into two parts the Tool Organizer features five sliding drawers and a compartment specially designed to securely hold large size hand tools such as hammers and screwdrivers.

Zucchetti

Italy

Zucchetti
Rubinetteria S.p.A.

Via Molini di Resiga, 29
28024 Gozzano
Tel. +39 0322 95 47 00
Fax +39 0322 95 47 23
marketing@zucchettirub.it
www@zucchettionline.it

Founded in Valduggia in 1929 by Alfredo Zucchetti, Zucchetti Rubinetteria S.p.A. relocated to Gozzano (Novara), still today the official location of the company, in 1939. Conversion to sanitary ware took place in 1946, when Mario Zucchetti (son of Alfredo Zucchetti), the current chairman, joined the firm. The solid family business tradition is maintained with the presence of the third generation: Carlo and Elena Zucchetti, brother and sister, and the cousins Marco and Paolo Zucchetti, joint owners of Zucchetti Rubinetteria S.p.A. The success of Zucchetti products is seen by the company as a result of its policy of investing in R&D, and above all of the decision to work with well-known design engineers, architects and designers, to offer state of the art products both in technology and choice of materials and in a design inspired by new trends. Since the year 2000, in particular, Zucchetti Rubinetteria S.p.A. has benefited from contributions from one of the most famous and sought-after architects and designers in the world, Matteo Thun and his design firm. Matteo Thun, with Antonio Rodriguez for the design and Elena Mattei for the graphics, have worked together with the company in designing and creating the isy* by Zucchetti range. This is an innovative system, with the technical novelty of a totally concealed mixer.

It is no coincidence that the isystick single control mixer is patent pending. With isy* by Zucchetti, the company confirms its top ranking in the area of production of taps. The company, with its extensive sales network formed by over 500 retailers in Italy, has achieved an outstanding position on the world market, exporting its products to more than 100 countries worldwide: France, Spain, Germany, England and Belgium, and also to non-European countries such as Mexico, Canada, China, Hong Kong and Australia.

Zucchetti Rubinetteria S.p.A. is part of a group formed by three other companies: Zucchetti Mario S.p.A. for the press-forging of brass, Omez for the moulding of plastics and Zucchetti Engineering for the design and manufacture of moulds for the mechanical engineering industry. To date the group boasts 4 technologically advanced plants and a distribution unit where 500 highly specialised operatives work. The Zucchetti group combines the advantages of a large, standardised traditional company and those of a more flexible corporation, with a strong drive towards innovation and exports, managerial flexibility and fast decisions. With quality at the core of its entire corporate philosophy, Zucchetti obtained certification of its quality system to the UNI EN ISO 9001 standard as far back as 1995.

isystick: "Something different, not a change in shape, but a new way of controlling water": that was the brief from Zucchetti to Matteo Thun at their first meeting. isy* was the answer. "Not a new tap, but a system which speaks the language of simplicity to a polyglot public", said Matteo Thun, "not a design process, but an idea designed by water". The other strong idea in the isy* design is modularity. A single rose design produces all the spout solutions and all the control functions: the joystick for the single-control system and three types of handles for the traditional tap system. A few basic parts create five product ranges: isystick, isyline, isyarc, isycontract and isybagno, each with its special features of line and design, but all sharing a single idea: a basic shape designed by the plasticity of the water.

isystick. single-lever mixer: This is a complete range of single-lever mixers with the cartridge positioned below the ceramic top. The cartridge has sintered ceramic disks, certified to the American standard ANSI/NSF 61 "Drinking water system components - health effects". The body is in brass and the spout can be removed and replaced with a fast pressure-hooking system. isystick is available with a chromed finished with a control lever in chrome, blonde or dark wood, or black shellac.

Austria

Zumtobel Staff

Zumtobel Staff GmbH

Schweizer Strasse 30
6850 Dornbirn
Tel. +43 5572 390-0
Fax +43 5572 22 826
info@zumtobelstaff.co.at
www.zumtobelstaff.com

Creating worlds of experience with light – in offices and education, industry and technology, presentation and retail, art and culture, hotels and restaurants, sport and leisure, health and care: that is the Zumtobel Staff philosophy, that is the vision of the Dornbirn-based Austrian company founded in 1950, and that is the challenge taken up by its workforce of about 3,000 employees around the globe on a daily basis.

As an internationally successful manufacturer with many decades of experience in providing luminaires and project-based lighting solutions, Zumtobel Staff believes that the lighting experience should always be interpreted as the effort to achieve an awareness of form as well as perfection in creative design – irrespective of whether that involves exclusive office luminaires for the directors' suite or continuous row systems for manufacturing premises, downlights and spotlight systems for the flagship stores of renowned fashion designers or surface-mounted luminaires for the supermarket around the corner, spotlights for museums and exhibition halls in the metropolitan art centres of this world or illuminated escape signs to point the way to emergency exits in hotels and hospitals. Product design is never an end in itself. The formal language of a luminaire must be developed and articulated as part of a dialogue with its technological features and their photometric characteristics. Form follows function – a Bauhaus dictum into which Zumtobel Staff constantly breathes new life: not least through the many years of productive and ambitious collaboration with internationally renowned designers which has proved to be highly successful, as borne out by the many design prizes regularly awarded to Zumtobel Staff luminaires. Because ultimately the lighting systems which have resulted from these partnerships demonstrate that the perfect combination of optimal lighting quality, the capacity for technological innovation as well as aesthetically and functionally stunning design is what determines the creative power of light: light which elicits a response, which appeals to the intellect, the senses and the emotions. Light which is an integral part of architecture. Light which creates worlds of experience.

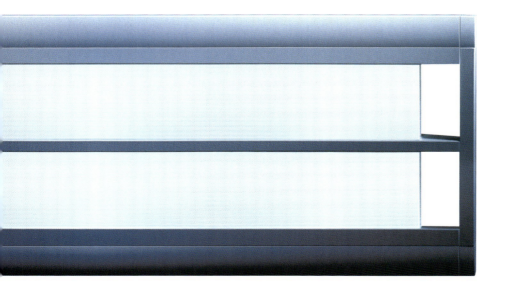

Aero: In the case of the innovative waveguide lighting technology of the pendant luminaire Aero, Sottsass Associati faced the difficult challenge of radically rethinking the office luminaire and creating a design which would provide the right expression for this new quality of light distribution in terms of both shape and form.

Xeno: The basic shapes of the cube and the cylinder, linked by a striking X joint, are the basis for the unmistakable design concept which Jean-Michel Wilmotte has developed for the spotlight system Xeno, the ideal choice for professional lighting design solutions in museums, galleries, shops and stores.

ICSID

ICSID – A Global Network for Design

ICSID's influence reaches across the globe. Its activities have an impact wherever they occur – whether in industrialised western economies, or, increasingly, in those parts of the developing world where the need for design is predicated, not so much by the demands of a mature market economy, but rather, by social need.

Through its international Congresses, which are organised and hosted by member societies in different parts of the world, ICSID continues to contribute to the long line of thinking and debate about the role and purpose, as well as the changing nature, of design.

These major events, which take place every two years, act as a focus for design at the international level and provide an opportunity for members to build professional contacts and extend the ever-growing network. With up to 1000 delegates, the Congresses are recognised as an established and significant contribution to the calendar of the many disparate design events which take place across continents. Traditionally, the Congresses conclude with the two-day ICSID General Assembly. Business administration and management issues are the main items on the agenda of the Assembly. Council Members also vote on current international issues and elect the new Executive Board.

ICSID Interdesigns offer nations a unique opportunity to bring together outstanding designers and design educators from across the world, to work together in intensive two week workshops, on pressing design issues. Developing solutions around problems of regional or international significance, such as, for example, the provision of clean water in many parts of the African Continent, offers a chance to raise the profile of design in a region, to drive towards sustainable solutions and to increase the visibility of the local ICSID members.

This is also true for ICSID Regional Meetings which are organised and hosted by ICSID members, in collaboration with local organisers and supported by the ICSID Executive Board and Secretariat. These events allow local problems and issues, such as a lack of design policy at the national level or a low uptake of design by local industry, to be addressed.

ICSID also endorses international design events, to demonstrate that they have been organised in accordance with approved international guidelines and standards. As part of its communications programme, ICSID issues the bimonthly ICSIDnews which reports on international developments in industrial design, acts as a platform for the discussion of topical issues for design, and provides information on ICSID activities. Other

• Locations of the member organisations of ICSID

publications include the World Directory of Industrial Design Education and the bimonthly ICSID Calendar, showing international design projects, exhibitions, competitions, seminars, conferences and endorsed events.

Based in Helsinki, the ICSID Secretariat oversees the daily activities of the Council. It is responsible for supporting the ICSID membership and the ICSID Executive Board, which meets four times a year. The Secretariat is also responsible for managing the organisation's finances, advising member societies on the organisation of various ICSID endorsed events, as well as producing the ICSIDnews and ICSID Calendar update.

Mrs. Kaarina Pohto has been Secretary General of ICSID since 1985 and was formerly Director of the Finnish Association of Designers from 1982 to 1993. She graduated from the Helsinki School of Economics, Finland, acted as Secretary General of the joint ICOGRADA / ICSID / IFI Design 1981 Congress in Helsinki, and is an Honorary Member of the Finnish Association of Designers, ORNAMO.

ICSID Secretariat
Erottajankatu 11 A 18
00130 Helsinki
Finland
Tel: +358 9 696 22 90
Fax: +358 9 696 22 910
icsidsec@icsid.org

The Executive Boards

At a design conference initiated by Jacques Vienot and hosted by the Institut d´Ésthetique Industrielle Paris in 1955, the delegation decided to establish an international organisation of industrial design and adopted "International Committee of Industrial Design Societies" as a provisional name. The delegates subsequently met at the Royal Institute of British Architects in London June 27-29, 1957 and agreed to establish ICSID, The International Council of Societies of Industrial Design.

ICSID consists of an Executive Board, an Advisory Senate, Regional Advisors, Member Societies and affiliated organisations. These bodies work together in the areas of professional practice, education, promotion and development to enhance both the ways designers work and the contexts within which they practice.

The ICSID Executive Board consists of 11 individuals including the President, the President-Elect, and 9 Board Members. Executive Board Members donate their time and expertise freely to further ICSID's mandate. The Executive Board is elected every two years by the ICSID General Assembly, and is chiefly responsible for managing all ICSID business. The Treasurer, an honorary position, is selected by the newly elected Board during their first meeting, immediately following the closing of the General Assembly. Over the years, numerous boards have defined their priorities, together contributing to the wide range of tools and activities available to ICSID today. The membership of all ICSID Executive Boards is listed on the following pages.

ICSID Executive Board 1957 – 1959

Mr. Peter Muller-Munk	**President**
Sir Misha Black	Executive Vice President
Mr. Enrico Peressuti	Vice President
Mr. Pierre Vago	Secretary Treasurer
Count Sigvard Bernadotte	Board Member

ICSID Executive Board 1959 – 1961

Sir Misha Black	**President**
Mr. Peter Muller-Munk	Past President
Ms. Mia Seeger	Secretary Treasurer
Count Sigvard Bernadotte	Vice President
Mr. Pierre Vago	Vice President
Mr. Enrico Peressuti	Board Member

ICSID Executive Board 1961 – 1963

Count Sigvard Bernadotte	**President**
Sir Misha Black	Past President
Ms. Mia Seeger	Secretary Treasurer
Mr. Jay Doblin	Vice President
Mr. Alberto Rosselli	Vice President
Mr. Pierre Vago	Board Member

ICSID Executive Board 1963 – 1965

Mr. Pierre Vago	**President**
Count Sigvard Bernadotte	Past President
Sir Paul Reilly	Honorary Treasurer
Mr. George Beck	Vice President
Mr. John Radic	Vice President
Mr. Andre Ricard	Vice President
Mrs. Josine des Cressonnières	Secretary General
Mr. Marco Zanuso	Board Member

ICSID Executive Board 1965 – 1967

Mr. Richard S. Latham	**President**
Sir Paul Reilly	Honorary Treasurer
Mr. John Radic	Vice President
Mr. André Ricard	Vice President
Mr. Karl Schwanzer	Vice President
Mrs. Josine des Cressonnières	Secretary General
Mr. Tomas Maldonado	Board Member
Mr. Jacques S. Guillon	Board Member

ICSID Executive Board 1967 – 1969

Mr. Tomas Maldonado	**President**
Mr. Richard S. Latham	Past President
Mr. Jacques S. Guillon	Treasurer
Mr. Ulf Hård af Segerstad	Vice President
Mr. Andrzej Pawlowski	Vice President
Mr. Gino Valle	Vice President
Mrs. Josine des Cressonnières	Secretary General
Mr. Eliot Noyes	Board Member
Mr. John Reid	Board Member

ICSID Executive Board 1969 – 1971

Mr. John Reid	**President**
Mr. Henri Vienot	Honorary Treasurer
Mr. Ulf Hård af Segerstad	Vice President
Mr. Eliot Noyes	Vice President
Dr. Yuri Soloviev	Vice President
Mr. Gino Valle	Vice President
Mrs. Josine des Cressonnières	Secretary General
Mr. Edgar Kaufmann Jr.	Board Member
Mr. Andrzej Pawlowski	Board Member
Mr. Carl Auböck	Board Member
Mr. André Ricard	Board Member

ICSID Executive Board 1971 - 1973

Mr. Henri Vienot	**President**
Mr. John Reid	Past President
Mr. Jurgen Hämer	Honorary Treasurer
Mr. Carl Auböck	Vice President
Dr. Yuri Soloviev	Vice President
Mr. André Ricard	Vice President
Mrs. Josine des Cressonnières	Secretary General
Mr. Rodolfo Bonetto	Board Member
Mr. Frank Dudas	Board Member
Mr. Kenji Ekuan	Board Member

ICSID Executive Board 1973 - 1975

Mr. Carl Auböck	**President**
Mr. Henri Vienot	Past President
Mr. Jurgen Hämer	Honorary Treasurer
Mr. Rodolfo Bonetto	Vice President
Mr. Gui Bonsiepe	Vice President
Mr. Kenji Ekuan	Vice President
Mrs. Josine des Cressonnières	Secretary General
Mr. Richard Hollerith	Board Member
Mr. Martin Kelm	Board Member
Mr. Juhani Salovaara	Board Member
Mr. Richard Stevens	Board Member

ICSID Executive Board 1975 – 1977

Mr. Kenji Ekuan	**President**
Mr. Carl Auböck	Past President
Mr. Richard Stevens	Treasurer
Mr. Richard Hollerith	Vice President
Ms. Mary Mullin	Vice President
Dr. Yuri Soloviev	Vice President
Mrs. Josine des Cressonnières	Secretary General
Mr. Herbert Ohl	Board Member
Mr. Wolfgang Schmidt	Board Member
Mr. Jan Trägårdh	Board Member

ICSID Executive Board 1977 - 1979

Dr. Yuri Soloviev	**President**
Mr. Kenji Ekuan	Past President
Mr. Herbert Ohl	Honorary Treasurer
Prof. Arthur J. Pulos	Vice President
Mr. André Ricard	Vice President
Mr. Jan Trägårdh	Vice President
Mr. Yoshio Nishimoto	Secretary General
Mr. Ryszard Bojar	Board Member
Mr. Dirk Jacobs	Board Member
Ms. Francoise Jollant	Board Member
Mr. Wolfgang Schmidt	Board Member

ICSID Executive Board 1979 - 1981

Prof. Arthur J. Pulos	**President**
Dr. Yuri Soloviev	Past President
Mr. Alejandro Lazo Margain	Honorary Treasurer
Mr. Ryszard Bojar	Vice President
Ms. Carla Venosta	Vice President
Mr. Loek van der Sande	Secretary General
Mr. Dirk Jacobs	Board Member
Ms. Francoise Jollant	Board Member
Prof. Antti Nurmesniemi	Board Member
Mr. H.K. Vyas	Board Member
Mr. Knut Yran	Board Member

ICSID Executive Board 1981 - 1983

Mr. Rodolfo Bonetto	**President**
Prof. Arthur J. Pulos	Past President
Mr. Ekkehard Bartsch	Honorary Treasurer
Mr. Arthur Goldreich	Vice President
Mr. Kazuo Kimura	Vice President
Mr. Loek van der Sande	Secretary General
Mr. Alejandro Lazo Margain	Board Member
Mr. Peter Lord	Board Member
Mr. Terje Meyer	Board Member
Prof. Antti Nurmesniemi	Board Member
Mr. Jean-Claude Fenaux	Board Member

ICSID Executive Board 1983 – 1985

Mr. Loek van der Sande — President
Mr. Rodolfo Bonetto — Past President
Mr. Ekkehard Bartsch — Honorary Treasurer
Mr. Peter Lord — Secretary General
Dr. Robert Blaich — Vice President
Mr. Kazuo Kimura — Vice President
Mr. Terje Meyer — Board Member
Mr. Keith Grant — Board Member
Mr. Richard Collins — Board Member
Mr. Antti Siltavuori — Board Member
Mr. Deane W. Richardson — Board Member
Mr. Jean-Claude Fenaux — Board Member

ICSID Executive Board 1985 – 1987

Mr. Peter Lord — President
Mr. Loek van der Sande — Past President
Dr. Robert Blaich — Secretary General
Mr. Antti Siltavuori — Honorary Treasurer
Mr. Pere Aguirre — Vice President
Mr. Alexander Neumeister — Vice President
Mr. Richard Collins — Board Member
Mr. Keith Grant — Board Member
Prof. Danielle Quarante — Board Member
Mr. Zoltán Szabó — Board Member
Mr. Nils J. Tvengsberg — Board Member

ICSID Executive Board 1987 – 1989

Dr. Robert Blaich — President
Mr. Peter Lord — Past President
Dr. Wolfgang Swoboda — Treasurer
Ms. Anne-Marie Boutin — Vice President
Mr. Vinay Jha — Vice President
Mr. Nils J. Tvengsberg — Vice President
Mr. Shoji Ekuan — Board Member
Ms. June Fraser — Board Member
Prof. Sasa Mächtig — Board Member
Mr. Deane W. Richardson — Board Member
Mr. Zoltán Szabó — Board Member

ICSID Executive Board 1989 – 1992

Prof. Antti Nurmesniemi — President
Dr. Robert Blaich — Past President
Dr. Wolfgang Swoboda — Treasurer
Ms. Anne-Marie Boutin — Board Member
Mr. Paul Y.J. Cheng — Board Member
Mr. Angelo Cortesi — Board Member
Dr. Mai Felip-Hösselbarth — Board Member
Ms. June Fraser — Board Member
Mr. András Mengyán — Board Member
Prof. Sasa Mächtig — Board Member
Mr. Deane W. Richardson — Board Member

ICSID Executive Board 1992 – 1993

Mr. Deane W. Richardson — President
Prof. Antti Nurmesniemi — Past President
Mr. Uwe Bahnsen — Treasurer
Mr. Jens Bernsen — Board Member
Mr. Paul Y.J. Cheng — Board Member
Mr. Angelo Cortesi — Board Member
Dr. Mai Felip-Hösselbarth — Board Member
Mr. Alexander Manu — Board Member
Mr. Kazuo Morohoshi — Board Member
Prof. Dr. h.c. Dieter Rams — Board Member
Mr. Gianfranco Zaccai — Board Member

ICSID Executive Board 1993 – 1995

Dr. Mai Felip-Hösselbarth — President
Mr. Deane W. Richardson — Past President
Mr. Uwe Bahnsen — Treasurer
Mr. Sannie Abdul — Board Member
Mr. Jens Bernsen — Board Member
Mr. Alexander Manu — Board Member
Mr. Kazuo Morohoshi — Board Member
Mr. Eduardo Barroso Neto — Board Member
Prof. Dr. h.c. Dieter Rams — Board Member
Dr. Zbynek Vokrouhlicky — Board Member
Mr. Gianfranco Zaccai — Board Member

ICSID Executive Board 1995-1997

Mr. Uwe Bahnsen	President
Dr. Mai Felip-Hösselbarth	Past President
Mr. Fritz Frenkler	Treasurer
Mr. Eduardo Barroso Neto	Board Member
Dr. Zdenka Yousefzamany-Burianova	Board Member
Dr. Kyung-won Chung	Board Member
Dr. Jorge Gómez Abrams	Board Member
Mr. Jan Lucassen	Board Member
Prof. Augusto Morello	Board Member
Mr. Kiyoshi Sakashita	Board Member
Ms. Adrienne Viljoen	Board Member

ICSID Executive Board 1997-1999

Prof. Augusto Morello	President
Mr. Uwe Bahnsen	Past President
Mr. Fritz Frenkler	Treasurer
Mr. Peter Butenschøn	Board Member
Dr. Kyung-won Chung	Board Member
Mr. Luigi Ferrara	Board Member
Dr. Jorge Gómez Abrams	Board Member
Mr. Theo J.J. Groothuizen	Board Member
Mr. David Kusuma	Board Member
Assoc. Prof. Vesna Popovic	Board Member
Ms. Adrienne Viljoen	Board Member

ICSID Executive Board 1999-2001

Prof. Augusto Morello	President
Mr. Peter Butenschøn	President Elect
Mr. Soon-In Lee	Treasurer
Mr. Manuel Alvarez-Fuentes	Board Member
Mr. Luigi Ferrara	Board Member
Mr. Theo J.J. Groothuizen	Board Member
Mr. Tapani Hyvönen	Board Member
Mr. David Kusuma	Board Member
Prof. Ron Nabarro	Board Member
Assoc. Prof. Vesna Popovic	Board Member
Prof. Dr. Peter Zec	Board Member

ICSID Executive Board 2001-2003

Mr. Peter Butenschøn, Norway	President

Mr. Luigi Ferrara, Canada	President Elect

Mr. Soon-In Lee, Korea	Treasurer

Mrs. Marianne Frandsen, Denmark	Board Member

Prof. Carlos Hinrichsen, Chile	Board Member

Mr. Tapani Hyvönen, Finland	Board Member

Prof. Ron Nabarro, Israel	Board Member

Dr. Darlie O. Koshy, India	Board Member

Prof. George Teodorescu, Germany	Board Member

Mr. Michael Thomson, United Kingdom	Board Member

Prof. Dr. Peter Zec, Germany	Board Member

Mrs. Kaarina Pohto, Finland	Secretary General 1985-2003

The ICSID Senate consists of the Past Presidents of the ICSID Executive Board. The outgoing President automatically becomes an ICSID Senator and will serve as Convenor of the Senate for the following term of office. Acting as an advisory board, the Senators contribute a broad range of knowledge and experience to the ongoing development of ICSID. The immediate Past President, Convenor of the Senate, acts as the liaison between the Senate and the current ICSID Executive Board.

Recent issues in which the Senate has been actively involved include constitutional amendments, a definition of industrial design, a code of professional practice and collaboration with affiliate organisations.

The members of the ICSID Senate are:

Prof. Augusto Morello, Italy († 2002)
ICSID President 1997-2001

Mr. Uwe Bahnsen, Switzerland
ICSID President 1995-1997

Dr. Mai Felip-Hösselbarth, Spain
ICSID President 1993-1995

Mr. Deane W. Richardson, USA
ICSID President 1992-1993

Prof. Antti Nurmesniemi, Finland
ICSID President 1989-1992

Dr. Robert Blaich, USA
ICSID President 1987-1989

Mr. Peter Lord, United Kingdom
ICSID President 1985-1987

Mr. Loek van der Sande, The Netherlands
ICSID President 1983-1985

Mr. Yuri B. Soloviev, Russian Federation
ICSID President 1977-1979

Mr. Kenji Ekuan, Japan
ICSID President 1975-1977

Professional Members

Design Institute of Australia, DIA
196 Flinders Street
GPO Box 4352QQ
Melbourne, VIC 3001
Australia
dia@vecci.org.au

Asociacion Chilena de Empresas de Diseño – Chilean Design Association, QVID (pf)
Avda. santa Maria 0120
Providencia
Santiago
Chile
merq@ctcinternet.cl

Finnish Association of Designers, ORNAMO
Unioninkatu 26
FIN-00130 Helsinki
Finland
office@ornamo.fi

Design Austria, DA
Kandlgasse 16
A-1070 Vienna
Austria
info@designaustria.at

Croatian Design Society /Hrvatsko drustvo dizajnera, HDD
Dezelicev prilaz 20
10 000 Zagreb
Croatia
secretariat@cro-design.org

Verband Deutscher Industrie-Designer e.v., VDID
Gelsenkirchener Str. 181
45309 Essen
Germany
ddv@germandesign.de

Association of Applied Artists and Designers of Bosnia and Herzegovina, ULUPUBIH
Centar Skenderija
"Collegium Artisticum"
71000 Sarajevo
Terezije b.b.
Bosnia and Herzegovina
apluidbh@bih.net.ba

Association of Danish Designers/Föreningen Danske Designere MDD
Frederiksberggade 26, 4. sal
DK-1459 Copenhagen K
Denmark
mdd@mdd.dk

Association of Hungarian Fine Artists, AHFA
Postafiok 51
1364 Budapest
Hungary
studio@paqart.hu

Association of Canadian Industrial Designers, ACID
360 Place Royale, Suite 3
Montréal, Québec
H2Y 2V1
Canada
adiq@sympatico.ca

Estonian Society of Designers, ESD
Design Institute, Tallinn Art Academy
Tartu mnt. 1
EE-0001 Tallinn
Estonia

Society of Industrial Designers in India, SIDI
Care K-6, Rizvi Park
S.V. Road, Santacruz West
Mumbai 400 054
India

Institute of Designers in Ireland, IDI
8 Merrion Square
Dublin 2
Ireland
brewster@iol.ie

Korea Association of Industrial Design, KAID
757-1 Pangbae Dong
2nd Floor, Hansem Building
Seocho Ku
Seoul 137-060
Korea
master@kaid.or.kr

Norwegian Industrial Designers, NID
Mariboesgt 11
N-0183 Oslo
Norway
info@nid.no

Design South Africa, DSA
P.O. Box 84288
Greenside
Johannesburg 2034
Republic of South Africa
dsa@liberty.co.za

China Industrial Designers Association, CIDA
6F-1, 99, Jen Ai, Road
Section 4, Taipei 106
Taiwan, China
service@cida.org.tw

Israel Industrial Designers Association, IIDA
c/o Studio Shacham
Moshav Sede Warburg 44935
Israel
shachams@netvision.net.il

Latvian Designers' Society, LDS
5a Gertrudes Street
LV-1010 Riga
Republic of Latvia
lia@index.apollo.lv

Stow. Projektantów Form Przemystowych, SPFP
Skr. poczt. 14
00-975 Warsaw 12
Poland

Asociació de Disseny Industrial del FAD, ADI-FAD
FAD-Foment de Les Arts Decoratives
Plaça dels Angels, 5-6
08001 Barcelona
Spain
adifad@adi-fad.ictnet.es

Industrial Designers Society of Thailand, IDST
c/o Office of Prod. Devel. & Design for Export -
Dept of Export Promotion
22/77 Ratchadapisek Rd.
Chatuchak
Bangkok 10900
Thailand
info@ids.or.th

Associazione per il Disegno Industriale, ADI
via Bramante, 29
I-20154 Milan
Italy
adi@essai.it

Beroepsorganisatie Nederlandse Ontwerpers, BNO
Weesperstraat 5
1018 DN Amsterdam
The Netherlands
bno@bno.nl

Romanian Atists' Union - Design Department, RAU-DD
Str. Nicolae Iorga 21
Bucharest 71117
Romania
uap@dnt.ro

The Society of Swedish Industrial Designers, SID
Industrihuset
Storgatan 19
Box 5501
SE-114 85 Stockholm
Sweden
info@sid.se

Industrial Designers Society of America, IDSA
45195 Business Court, Suite 250
Dulles, VA 20166-6717
USA
idsa@idsa.org

Japan Industrial Designers' Association, JIDA
International Relation Committee
Axis Building 2F
17-1 Roppongi, 5-Chome
Minato-ku
Tokyo 106-0032
Japan
jidasec@jida.or.jp

Designers Institute of New Zealand Inc. DINZ
Box 5521
Wellesley Street
Auckland
New Zealand
designer@dinz.org.nz

Designers' Society of Slovenia, DOS
Ciril Metodov trg 19
SL-1000 Ljubljana
Slovenia

Swiss Design Association, SDA
Weinbergstrasse 31
CH-8006 Zürich
Switzerland
sda@amsnet.ch

Professional / Promotional Members

Form Island
c/o Ministry of Education, Science and Culture
Sölvholsgata 4
140 Reykjavik
form.island@itn.is

Asociación de Diseñadores Industriales de Guadalajara A C, ASDIG
Luis Perez Verdía 122 A, S.H.
C.P. 44600
Guadalajara, Jal.
Mexico
camaleon@vianet.com.mx

Scientific and Research Institute for Technic and Aestetique, VNIITE
Exposition Centre of Russia
Building 115
129223 Moscow
Russian Federation

Promotional Members

Australian Design
Awards, ADA
286 Sussex Street
Sydney NSW 2000
Australia
ada@standards.com.au

National Design Center,
NDC
34 Totleben Blvd.
1606 Sofia BG
Republic of Bulgaria

Oficina Nacional de
Diseño Industrial, ONDI
Calle 47 #3446
Rpto. Kholy, Playa
Ciudad de la Habana,
11300
Cuba
cuendias@ondi.cu

Vlaams Instituut voor het
Zelfstandig Ondernemen,
VIZO
Kanselarijstraat 19
1000 Brussels
Belgium
johan.valcke@vizo.be
info@vizo.be

Design Exchange, DX
234 Bay Street
P.O. Box 18
Toronto-Dominion Centre
Toronto, Ontario
M5K 1B2
Canada
luigi@dxnet.net

Design Centrum of the
Czech Republic, DCCR
Radnická 2
602 00 Brno
Czech Republic

Associação de
Ensino/Pesquisa de Nível
Superior em Design do
Brasil, AEnD-BR
Av. Epitácio Pessoa 1664,
3rd Fl. Ipanema
Rio de Janeiro, RJ
22471-030
Brazil
aend-br@univercidade.br

Institut de Design
Montréal, IDM
390, rue St. Paul East,
Suite 300
Montréal, Québec
H2Y 1H2
Canada
idm@idm.qc.ca

Pracoviste Praha
Sekaninova 40
128 00 Prague 2
Czech Republic
vok@designcentrum.cz

Fed. das Indústriales
do Estado do São Paulo,
FIESP/CIESP
Avenida Paulista, 1313-
5th floor
01311-923 São Paulo - SP
Brazil
flongo@fiesp.org.

Artesanías de Colombia
S.A., ACSA
Carrera 3
No. 18-60
Bogotá
Colombia
intcoop@colomsat.net.co

Danish Design
Council/Danish Design
Centre, DDC
H C Andersen Boulevard 27
1553 Copenhagen V
Denmark
design@ddc.dk

Design Forum Finland, DFF
Erottajankatu 15-17 A
FIN-00130 Helsinki
Finland
info@designforum.fi

German Design Council /
Rat Für Formgebung, RfF
Rat-Haus, Messegelände
Ludwig-Erhanrd-Anlage 1
Postfach 15 03 11
D-60063 Franfurt/Main
Germany
info@german-design-council.de

National Institute of Design, NID
Paldi
Ahmedabad 380 007
India
info@nid.edu
edoffice@nid.edu

Malaysia Design Council, MRM
Suite G-04, Ground floor
207 Jalan Tun Razak
50 400 Kuala Lumpur
Malaysia
mdc@malaysiadesign-council.gov.my

Norsk Form, NF
Kongens gate 4
N-0153 Oslo
Norway
peter.butenschon@norsk-form.no

Agence pour la Promotion de la Création Industrielle, APCI
24 rue du Charolais
75012 Paris
France
info@apci.asso.fr

Industrie Forum Design Hannover, iF
Messegelände
D-30521 Hannover
Germany
info@ifdesign.de

Japan Design Foundation, JDF
3-1-800 Umeda
1-Chome, Kita-ku
Osaka 530-0001
Japan
jdf@silver.ocn.ne.jp

Malaysia Design Technology Centre, MDTC
No. 1, Jalan SS26/2
Taman Mayang Jaya
47301 Petaling Jaya
Selongor Darul Ehsan
Malaysia
enquiry@mdtc.com.my

Norwegian Design Council, NDC
Industriens Hus
Oscarsgate20
Postboks 5322 Majorstua
N-0304 Oslo
Norway
jrs@norskdesign.no

Design Center Stuttgart, DCS
Landesgewerbeamt
Baden-Württemberg
Haus der Wirtschaft
Willy-Bleicher-Str. 19
D-70174 Stuttgart
Germany
design@lgabw.de

Hungarian Council of Industrial Design and Ergonomics, IFET
1370 Budapest 5
POB 552
Hungary
lakatos@hpo.hu

Japan Industrial Design Promotion Organization, JIDPO
4th Floor, Annex, World Trade Center
2-4-1 Hamamtsu-cho
Minato-ku
Tokyo 105 6190
Japan
p-div@jidpo.or.jp

Mexico Design Promotion Center, CPDM
Av. Insurgentes Sur 1855
Piso 10
Col. Guadalupe Inn
01020 Mexico, D.F.
Mexico
cpdm@centrodiseno.com

Product Development and Design Center, PDDCP
Cultural Center Complex
Roxas Boulevard,
Pasay City
Metro Manila 1300
Philippines
pddcp@mozcom.com

Design Zentrum Nordrhein Westfalen, DZ-NRW
Gelsenkirchener Str. 181
D-45309 Essen
Germany
info@dznrw.com

India Institute of Technology, Industrial Design Centre, IIT-IDC
IIT Powai
Mumbai 400-0076
India
office@idc.iitb.ac.in

Korea Institute of Design Promotion, KIDP
Korea Design Center/Bldg.7F
344-1 Yatap-dong
Bundang-gu, Seongnam City
Gyeonggi-do, Zip Code: 463-828
Korea
humaing@kidp.or.kr
kidp@kidp.or.kr

European Design Centre b.v., EDC
P.O. Box 6279
5600 HG Eindhovenn
The Netherlands
jmm@edc.nl

Singapore Trade Development Board Business Capability Division, DCS
230 Victoria Street #09-00
Bugis Junction Office Tower
Singapore 188024
Republic of Singapore
design@tdb.gov.sg

Slovak Design Centre, SDC
Jakubovo nám. 12
P.O. Box 131
814 99 Bratislava
Slovakia
sdc@sdc.sk

The Swedish Society of Crafts and Design / Föreningen Svensk Form, FSF
Holmamiralens vag 2
SE-111 49 Stockholm
Sweden

Design Institute - South African Bureau of Standards, DISABS
1 Dr. Lategan Road,
Groenkloof
Private Bag X191
Pretoria 0001
Republic of South Africa
viljoeab@sabs.co.za

China External Trade Development Council - Design Promotion Centre, CETRA
5th Floor, CETRA Tower
333 Keelung Road, Section 1
Taipei 110
Taiwan, China
design@cetra.org.tw

Barcelona Design Center, BCD
Av. Diagonal, 452-454,
5a pl.
E-08006 Barcelona
Spain
bcd@cambrabcn.es

China Productivity Center, CPC
Far East World Center,
C Block
2nd Floor, No. 79, Section 1
Hsin Tai Wu Road
Hsichi, Taipei Hsien 221
Taiwan, China
FrankPai@cpc.org.tw

The Swedish Industrial Design Foundation, SVID
Industrihuset
Storgatan 19
Box 5501
SE-114 85 Stockholm
Sweden
robin.edman@svid.se

Design Council, DC
34 Bow Street
London WC2E 7DL
United Kingdom
info@designcouncil.org.uk

Educational Members

Queensland University
of Technology, QUT
School of Design and Built
Environemnt
G.P.O. Box 2434
Gardens Point Campus
Brisbane Q 4001
Australia
v.popovic@qut.edu.au

Pontificia Universidad
Javeriana, Industrial
Design Career, PUJ-IDC
Carrera 7, No. 40-62
Ed. Carlos Arbeláez
Santafé de Bogotá 56710
Colombia
rcuervo@javeriana.edu.co

Université de Technologie
de Compiègne, UTC
Industrial Design
Department
Centre de Recherches
Pierre Guillaumat
B.P. 60319
60 206 Compiègne Cedex
France
anne.guenand@utc.fr

Universidade do Estado
do Rio de Janeiro, Escola
Superior de Desenho
Industrial, UERJ-ESDI
Rua Evaristo da Veiga 95
Rio de Janeiro
CEP 20031-040
Brazil
diretoria@esdi.uerj.br

Universidad Jorge Tadeo
LOZANO, UTADEO
Carrera 3 Esquina Calle 23
Edificio de Postgrados
Universidad Jorge Tadeo
Lozano
Bogota
Columbia
jorge.delcastillo@
utadeo.edu.co

State Academy of Art
and Design Stuttgart,
SAdbK-Stuttgart
Am Weiflenhof 1
D-70191 Stuttgart
Germany

Instituto Profesional
DUOC de la Universidad
Católica, DUOC-UC
School of Design
Darío Urzúa 2165
Providencia, Santiago
Chile
chinrichsen@duoc.cl

University of Art and
Design Helsinki, UIAH
Hämeentie 135 C
FIN-00560 Helsinki
Finland
yrjo.sotamaa@uiah.fi

The University of West
Hungary
Institute of Applied Art
Sopron , AMI
Deák ter 32.
9400 Sopron
Hungary
ami@fmk.nyme.hu

Les Ateliers, ENSCI
48, rue St. Sabin
75001 Paris
France
davis@ensci.com

Indian Institute of
Technology, Guwahati,
IIT-Guwahti
Department of Design
North Guwahati 781 031
Assam
India
nadkarni@iitg.ernet.in

Domus Academy –
Gruppo Webegg, DA
via Savona 97
I-20144 Milan
Italy
info@domac.it

Universidad
Iberoamericana, A.C., UIA
Prol. Paseo
de la Reforma 880
Lomas de Santa Fe
Mexico City
01210
Mexico

Institutt for
Produktdesign, NTNU
Kolbjørn Heies vei 2b
7491 Trondheim
Norway
per@design.ntnu.no

Shih-Chien University,
Institute of Industrial
Design, SCID
70 Ta-chi Street
Taipei 104
Taiwan, China
kuan@sccl.scc.edu.tw

Art Center College of
Design, ACCD
1700 Lida
Pasadena, CA 91001
USA
brucato@artcenter.edu

Yarmouk University
Fine Arts Department
Irbid 211-36
Jordan
qassl@yahoo.com

Delft University of
Technology
Faculty of Design,
Construction and
Production; OCP
Jaffalaan 9
2628 BX
Delft
The Netherlands
p.p.m.hekkert@io.tudelft.nl

Oslo School of
Architecture, Department
of Industrial Design, AHO
P.O. Box 6768
St. Olavs Plass
N-0130 Oslo
Norway
postmottak@aho.no

Istanbul Technical
University, ITU
Department of Industrial
Product Design
Faculty of Architecture
Taskisla Taksim
80191 Istanbul
Turkey
tasarim@itu.edu.tr

Carnegie Mellon
University, Department
of Design, CMU
110 Margaret Madison
Avenue
Pittsburgh, PA 15213-3890
USA
buchanan+@
andrew.cmu.edu

School of Engineering
and Architecture ITESM
Sucursal de Correos "J"
Monterrey, N.L. 64849
Mexico

The Design Academy
Eindhoven, AIVE
P.O. Box 2125
NL-5600 CC Eindhoven
The Netherlands
info@designacademy.nl
noks@designacademy.nl

Pontifical Catholic
University of Peru,
Faculty of Art, Product
Design Program, PUCP
Av. Universitaria Crda 18
San Miguel
Lima 32
Peru
mchamor@pucp.edu.pe

Middle East Technical
University, METU
Inönü Bulvari
06531 Ankara
Turkey
hasdogan@
arch.metu.edu.tr

Universidad Anahuac
School of Design, Anahuac
Av. Lomas Anahuac S/no.
Col, Lomas Anahuac
Huixquilucan, Edo. de
Mexico
C.P. 52760, Mexico
lamozu@anahuac.mx
mkorzenn@
orion.anahuac.mx

Akershus College
Department for Product
Design
Blaker Skanse
1925 Blaker
Norway
AlecAlan.Howe@hiak.no

Temasek Design School, TP
Temasek Polytechnic
21 Tampines Avenue 1
Singapore 529757
Singapore
alistairleung@tp.edu.sg

Mimar Sinan University,
MSÜ
Department of Industrial
Design
Meclis-i Mebusan Cad.
80040 Findikli
Istanbul
Turkey
endtas@msu.edu.tr

Associate Members

Diseño+Diseño, D+D
Av. Mitre 659
2nd Floor
Suites 1/13
5500 Mendoza
Argentina
ariasvl@lanet.com.ar

Bremer Design GmbH,
BDG
im Wilhelm Wagenfeld Haus
Am Wall 209
D-28195 Bremen
Germany
berthold@
designzentrumbremen.de

Centro Legno Arredo
Cantù, CLAC
piazza Garibaldi, 5
I-22063 Cantù
Italy
info@clac00.it

DesignCenter Brasil, DC
R. Dr. Flaquer 115 cj 53 B
Ibirapuera
04006-010
Sao Paulo - Sp
Brazil

Internationales Design
Zentrum Berlin e.v.,
IDZ Berlin
Rotherstrasse 16
D-10245 Berlin
Germany
idz@idz.de

Comitato Organizzatore
del Mobile Italiano,
COSMIT
Foro Buonaparte, 65
I-20121 Milan
Italy
espositori@isaloni.it

Design Innovation (HK)
Ltd., DI (HK)
LG1, HKPC Building
78 Tat Chee Avenue
Yau Yat Chuen
Kowloon
Hong Kong, China
designer@
design-innovation.com

International Institute of
Integral Design, IIID
Am Weißenhof 1
D-70191 Stuttgart
Germany
teodorescu@
integraldesign.de

Ente Gestione Mostre
Comufficio, SMAU
via Merano 18
I-20127 Milan, Italy
mktg@smau.it

Design Fr@nce (Centre
du Design Rhône-Alpes),
CDRA
9, rue Robert
69006 Lyon
France
gabillard@cdra.asso.fr

Indian Institute of Crafts
and Design, IICD
B-16/A, Bhawani Singh
Road
C-Scheme
Jaipur 302 005
Rajasthan
India
iicd@datainfosys.net

Marketing, Research &
Development s.r.l., MR&D
via Dante, 5
21013 Gallarate (Varese)
Italy
mrd@mrd-institute.com

International Design
Center NAGOYA Inc., IdcN
6 F, Design Center Bldg.
18-1, Sakae 3-Chome,
Naka-ku
Nagoya 460-0008
Japan
julia@idcnagoy.co.jp

Fundatio Romana Pentru
Design, FRD
Str. Dr. Mihail Petrini 8
Et. 1, Ap. 3, Sect. 5
Bucuresti
Romania
frdbuc@dnt.ro

As. Española de
Profesionales del Diseño,
AEPD
Rafael Calvo
28 bajo A
E-28010 Madrid
Spain
aepd@arrakis.es

Osaka Industrial Design
Center, OIDC
My-dome Osaka 4 Floor
2-5, Hommachibashi
Chuoku,
Osaka 540-0029
Japan
oidc@mbox.mydome.or.jp

Society of Designers
International Association,
SDIA
5 Bolshoy Kiselniy per.
103031 Moscow
Russian Federation

Centro de Diseño, DZ
Sabino Arana, 8
E-48013 Bilbao
Spain
centro@dzdesign.com

Design Society of Kenya,
DeSK
Department of Design
P.O.Box 30197
Nairobi
Kenya
mugendikm@yahoo.com

Biennial of Industrial
Design, BIO
BIO c/o AML
Karunova 4
SL-1000 Ljubljana
Slovenia
aml-bio@guest.arnes.si

Instituto Mediana y
Pequeña Industriales
Valenciana, IMPIVA
Plaza del Ayuntamiento, 6
E-46002 Valencia
Spain
amparo.sena@impiva.m400.gva.es

Portuguese Design
Center/Centro Português
de Design, CPD
Pólo Tecnológico de Lisboa
Lote 8
1600 -485 Lisboa
Portugal
info@cpdesign.pt

Information and
Documentation Centre
for Design , IDCO
Chamber of Economy
Dimiceva 13
1504 Ljubljana
Slovenia
maja.krzisnik@gzs.si

Soc. Estatal para el
Desarrollo del Diseño y la
Innovación, DDi
Paseo de la Castellana, 141,
1st Floor
E-28046 Madrid
Spain
info@se-ddi.es

Corporate Members

Alias|Wavefront, Alias
210 King Street East
Toronto, Ontario
M5A 1J7
Canada
awalsh@aw.sgi.com

Leitner GmbH
Exhibition systems
Düsseldorfer Straße 14
D-71332 Waiblingen
Germany
system@leitner.de

Toyota Motor
Corporation, TMC
Design Center
1, Toyota-cho
Toyota
Aichi 471-8572
Japan
nisimura@
design.en.toyota.co.jp

Fiskars Corporate Center,
FISKARS
Mannerheimintie 14 A
P.O. Box 235
FIN-00101 Helsinki
Finland
leena.kahilla-
bergh@fiskars.fi

MABEG Kreuschner
GmbH & Co. KG, MABEG
Ferdinand-Gabriel-Weg 10
D-59477 Soest
Germany
rainer.kranz@mabeg.de

Daewoo Electronics Co.
– Design Research Center
4th Floor, Shin Han
Building
12-3, Yoido-Dong
Yungdungpo-Gu
Seoul 150-010
Korea
ohosohn@web.dwe.co.kr

Nokia Mobile Phones,
NOKIA
Kelialahdentie 4
02150 Espoo
Finland
eero.miettinen@nokia.com

Alessi s.p.a. ALESSI
c/o F.A.O. s.p.a.
via Privata Alessi 6
I-28882 Crusinallo di
Omegna (VB)
Italy
info@alessi.com

Hanssem Co., Ltd
Hanssem Building 9th Floor
757-1 Bangbae-dong,
Seocho-gu
Seoul 137-060
Korea
yish@hanssem.co.kr

Braun GmbH, Braun
Frankfurter Str. 145
Postfach 1120
D-61476 Kronberg/Taunus
Germany
braun_design@gillette.com

Olivetti Tecnost Spa
via Lorenteggio 257
20100 Milano
Italy
c.rossanigo@
olivettilexikon.com

Hyundai Motor Company,
HMC
772-1 Jangduk-Dong
Whasung-Gun
Kyunggi-do 445-850
Korea
you@hmc.co.kr

LG Electronics Inc.
Digital Design Center, LGE
15th Floor
LG Kangnam Tower
679 Yuksaamdong,
Kangnam-ku
Seoul 135-080
Korea
chkim@lge.co.kr

HÅG a.s.a
Fritdtjof Nansens vei 12
P.O. Box 5055
N-0301 Oslo
Norway

Thomson multimedia Inc., TCE
10330 N. Meridian St. - INH-405
Indianapolis, IN 46290-1024
USA
ErberD@tce.com
grunwaldf@tce.com

Samsung Electronics Co., Ltd.
Corporate Design Center, Samsung CDC
12th Fl., Joong-ang Daily News Bldg.
7 Soonwha-dong,
Choong-ku
Seoul 100-750, Korea
ssylee@samsung.co.kr

Brown KSDP, KSDP
Private Bag X16
Sunninghill 2157
Republic of South Africa
kschilperoort@brownksdp.com
bwatt@brownksdp.com

Seongnam City Design Center
3F Venture Bld
587 Sujin 1-dong
Sujong-gu Seongnam City
Kyonggi-do0
Korea
kimys@lycos.co.kr

Tatung Co.
22 Chungshan North Road
Section 3
Taipei 10451
Taiwan, China

Philips Design, Philips
Building HWD
P.O. Box 218
Emmasingel 24
5600 MD Eindhoven
The Netherlands
Stefano.Marzano@philips.com

Design Management Institute, DMI
29 Temple Place, Second Floor
Boston, MA 02111-1350
USA
dmistaff@dmi.org

Companies

Special thanks are due to all these companies without whose support and provision of in-formation and photography, this book would not have been possible.

A

A&E Design AB
Rehnsgatan 11
S-11357 Stockholm
Sweden
Tel. +46 8 673 01 59
Fax +46 8 673 49 21
www.aedesign.se
page 32

AEG Hausgeräte GmbH
Muggenhofer Straße 135
D-90429 Nürnberg
Germany
Tel. +49 911 323-0
Fax +49 911 323-1770
www.aeg-hausgeraete.de
page 36

Alcatel Mobile Phone
32, Avenue Kléber
92707 Colombes Cedex
France
Tel. +33 155 66 34 12
Fax +33 155 66 74 95
www.alcatel.com
page 40

B

Blanco GmbH + Co KG
Flehinger Str. 59
75038 Oberderdingen
Germany
Tel. +49 7045 44-0
Fax +49 7045 44-299
info@blanco.de
www.blanco.de

Burkhard Leitner constructiv GnbH & Co.
Blumenstraße 36
70182 Stuttgart
Germany
Tel. +49 711 255 88-0
Fax +49 711 255 88-11
www.burkhardtleitner.de
page 42

C

Crown Equipment Corporation
44 South Washington St.
New Bremen, OH 45869
USA
Tel. +1 419 629-2311
Fax +1 419 629-3246
www.crown.com
page 44

D

DaimlerChrysler AG
70546 Stuttgart
Germany
Tel. +49 711 17-0
Fax +49 711 17-940 22
www.daimlerchrysler.com

DaimlerChrysler Corporation, USA
Auburn Hills, Michigan,
USA
MI 48326-2766
Tel. +1 248 576-57 41
Fax +1 248 576-47 42
page 46

Duravit AG
Werder Strasse 36
78132 Hornberg
Germany
Tel. +49 78331 70-0
Fax +49 78331 70-289
www.duravit.de
page 50

E

AB Electrolux
S:t Göransgatan 143
Stockholm
Sweden
Tel. +46 8 738 6000
Fax +46 8 738 4478
www.electrolux.com
page 54

F

Fiskars Consumer Oy Ab
Billnäs Fiskars
Consumer Oy Ab
Fin-10330 Billnäs
Finland
Tel. +358-19 / 277-721
Fax +358-19 / 236-350
www.fiskars.com
page 58

G

GRUPO D.I. S. DE R.L. DE C.V.
Altavista 119
Colonia San Angel Inn
01060 México D. F.
México
Tel. +52 55 616-07 70
Fax +52 55 550-64 97
www.grupodi.com
page 60

H

Herend Porcelain Manufactory Ltd.
Kossuth Layos St. 140
8440 Herend
Hungary
Tel. +36-88 / 523-100
Fax +36-88 / 261-518
www.herend.com
page 64

I

IBM Corporation
Route 100, CSB – CB 125
Somers, New York 10589
USA
Tel. +1 914 766-05 15
Fax +1 914 766-90 14
www.ibm.com
page 68

Iittala Designor Oy Ab
P.O. Box
FIN-00561 Helsinki
Finland
Tel. +358 204 39-11
Fax +358 204 39-57 42
www.iittala.fi
page 72

Intra AS
Storsand
N-7563 Malvik
Norway
Tel. +47 739 80-100
Fax +47 739 80-150
www.intra-group.com
page 74

Irizar S. Coop
Zumarraga Bidea, 8.
20216 Ormaiztegi
Gipuzkoa
Spain
Tel. +34 943 80 91 00
Fax +34 943 88 91 01
www.irizar.com
page 76

J

Jacob Jensen Design
Hejlskovvej 104
7840 Højslev
Denmark
Tel. +45 97 53 86 00
Fax +45 97 53 85 28
www.jacobjensen.com
page 78

K

Alfred Kärcher GmbH & Co.
Alfred Kärcher Straße 28 -40
71364 Winnenden
Germany
Tel. +49 7195 14-0
Fax +49 7195 14-22 12
www.kaercher.com
page 36

L

LG Electronics
Digital Design Center
LG Kangnam Tower 679
Yoksam-dong,Kangnam-gu,
135-080, Seoul
Korea
Tel. +82 2 20 05-31 10
Fax +82 2 20 05-31 15
www.lge.com
page 86

Ludwig Leuchten KG
Frühlingstraße 15
86415 Mering
Germany
Tel. +49 8233 387-0
Fax +49 8233 387-200
www.ludwig-leuchten.de
page 92

M

Mabeg Kreuschner GmbH & Co. KG
Ferdinand-Gabriel-Weg 10
59494 Soest
Germany
Tel. +49 2921 78 06-179
Fax +49 2921 78 06-177
www.mabeg.de
page 96

Makio Hasuike & Co
Via Pietro Custodi 16/A
20136 Milano
Italy
Tel. +39 02 58 10 31 93
Fax +39 02 58 10 23 11
www.makiohasuike.com
page 98

Miele & Cie. GmbH & Co.
Carl-Miele-Straße 29
33332 Gütersloh
Germany
Tel. +49 5241 89-0
Fax +49 5241 89-20 90
www.miele.de
page 100

Molteni & C. S.p.A.
Via Rossini 50
20034 Giussano
Italy
Tel. +39 0362 35 91
Fax +39 0362 355 170
www.molteni.it
page 102

Mono Mettalwarenfabrik Seibel GmbH
Industriestr. 5
40822 Mettmann
Germany
Tel. +49 2104 91 98 -0
Fax +49 2104 91 98 19
www.mono.com
page 104

N

Gebr. Niessing GmbH & Co.
Butenwall 117
48691 Vreden
Germany
Tel. +49 2564 300 -0
Fax +49 2564 300 -100
www.niessing.com
page 106

Nissan Motor Co., Ltd
17-1, Ginza 6-chome,
Vhuo-ku, Chuo-ku
Tokyo 104-8023
Japan
Tel. +81 3 55 65-21 41
Fax +81 3 35 46-26 69
www.nissan-global.com
page 108

Nya Nordiska Textiles GmbH
An den Ratswiesen
D-29451 Dannenberg
Germany
Fon + 49 5861 80 9-0
Fax + 49 5861 80 9-10
www.nya.com
page 114

O

O Luce s.r.l.
via Cavour, 52
20098 San Giuliano
Milanese - Milano
Italy
Tel. +39 02 98 49 14 35
Fax +39 02 98 49 07 79
www.oluce.com
page 118

P

Propagandist Co. Ltd.
779 /210
Pracharajbumphen Rd.
Samsennoak, Huay kwang
Bangkok / 10320
Thailand
Tel. +66 2 691-63 31
Fax +66 2 691-34 78
www.propagandaonline.de
page 120

R

Rado Watch Co. Ltd
Bielstrasse 45
2543 Lengnau
Switzerland
Tel. +41 32 655-61 11
Fax +41 32 655-61 12
www.rado.com
page 122

Randstad Holding nv
Diemermere 25
1112 TC Diemen
Netherlands
Tel. +31 20 569-5175
Fax +31 20 569-5630
www.randstad.com
page 128

S

Samsung Electronics Co., Ltd
Samsung Main Building
250-2ga, Taepyung-ro
Chung-gu, Seoul
Tel. +82 2 751-33 55
www.sec.co.kr
Corporate Design Center
14F, Joong-ang ilbo Bldg.,
7 Soonhwa-Dong,
Choong-Ku, Seoul
Korea 100-759
Tel. +82 2 750-92 96
Fax +82 2 750-94 25
www.samsungelectronics.com
page 134

Schwan-Stabilo Schwanhäußer GmbH & Co.
Schwanweg 1
90562 Heroldsberg
Germany
Tel. +49 911 567-0
Fax +49 911 567-44 44
www.stabilo.com
page 140

Sedus Stoll AG
Brückenstraße 15
79761 Waldshut
Germany
Tel. +49 7751 84 -0
Fax +49 7751 84 -3 10
www.sedus.de
page 142

Siemens-Elektrogeräte GmbH
Hochstrasse 17
81669 München
Germany
Tel. +49 89 45 90 - 09
Fax +49 89 45 90 - 23 47
www.siemens.com
page 144

Sony Corporation Tokyo
7-35, Kitashinagawa
6-chome
Shinagawa-ku
Tokyo 141-0001
Japan
Tel. +81 3 54 48 21 11
Fax +81 3 54 48 55 77
www.sony.net
page 146

Studio Idea Ltd.
Pl.Wilsona 4 m.54
01-627, Warszawa
Poland
Tel. +48 22 832 3391
Fax +48 22 832 3392
Mobile: +48 602 178589
studio@ideadesign.com.pl
page 152

T

TATA Engineering and Locomotive Co. Ltd.
Bombay House
24, Homi Mody Street
Hutatma Chowk,
Mumbai 400 001
India
Tel. +91 22 56 65 82 82
Fax +91 22 22 04 54 74
www.telcoindia.com
page 154

Toyota Motor Corporation
1 Toyota-Cho,
Aichi Prefecture
471-8571 Japan
Tel. +81 565 28 21 21
www.toyota.co.jp
page 156

Tupperware Corporation
Tupperware General
Services N. V. / Tupperware
Europe, Africa & Middle
East / Design Department
Pierre Corneliskaai 35
B-9300 Aalst
Belgium
Tel. 0032 53 72 75 41
Fax 0032 53 72 75 40
www.tupperware.com
page 162

V

Vivero Oy
Hämeentie 11
00530 Helsinki
Finland
Tel. +358 9 774-53 3-0
Fax +358 9 774-53 311
www.vivero.fi
page 166

Vorwerk & Co. KG
Mühlenweg 17-37
42270 Wuppertal
Germany
Tel. +49 202 56 40
Fax +49 202 56 43 271
www.vorwerk.de
page 170

Y

Yamaha Corporation
10-1 Nakazawa-cho
Hamamatsu City
Shizuoka Prefecture
Japan 430-8650
Tel. +81 53 460-28 83
Fax +81 53 463-49 22
www.global.yamaha.com
page 172

Z

ZAG Industries Ltd,
19 Ha'Melacha Street
New Industrial Zone
Rosh Ha'Ayin
48091
Israel
Tel. +972-3-90 20 200
Fax +972-3-90 20 222
www.zag.co.il
page 174

Zucchetti Rubinetteria S.p.A.
Via Molini di Resiga, 29
28024 Gozzano
Italy
Tel. +39 0322 95 47 00
Fax +39 0322 95 47 23
www@zucchettionline.it
page 178

Zumtobel Staff GmbH
Schweizer Straße 30
6850 Dornbirn
Austria
Tel. +43 5572 39 00
Fax +43 5572 22 826
www.zumtobelstaff.com
page 180

Acknowledgements: Many thanks are due to Mrs. Kaarina Pohto and the staff at the ICSID Secretariat for their kind assistance and cooperation.

Special thanks are also due to Michael Thomson, Principal of Design Connect (London) and a member of the current ICSID Executive Board, whose expert assistance accompanied this publication in all matters of content and editorial presentation.

Photographs: Special thanks are due to those companies which kindly provided photographic material for use in the first chapter of the book.

Apple Computer Inc., Cupertino (USA)
Braun GmbH, Kronberg (Germany)
British American Tobacco GmbH, Hamburg (Germany)
Coca-Cola GmbH, Essen (Germany)
DaimlerChrysler AG, Stuttgart (Germany)
Ford-Werke AG, Köln (Germany)
Vitra Design Museum, Weil am Rhein (Germany)

Hall of Fame
Companies Searching for Excellence in Design –
A Review of the 20th Century

Edited by Peter Zec on behalf of ICSID,
the International Council of Societies of Industrial
Design, Helsinki (Finland)
www.icsid.org

Idea: Professor Dr. Peter Zec
Editorial work: Burkhard Jacob on behalf of the
Design Zentrum Nordrhein Westfalen, Essen (Germany)
Cover and Layout: Prof. Uwe Loesch and Swen Hoppe
Proof reading and Translation: Lunn Drabble GmbH
Production, Lithography and Printing:
Rehrmann Plitt GmbH & Co. KG

Printed in Germany

reddot

German Publisher
ISBN 3-89939-060-1
red dot edition
Gelsenkirchener Strasse 181
45309 Essen, Germany
Tel. +49 201 30 10 4-34
Fax +49 201 30 10 4-40
info@red-dot.de
www.red-dot.de

Worldwide Distribution
ISBN 3-929638-79-7
avedition GmbH
Königsallee 57
71638 Ludwigsburg, Germany
Tel. +49 7141 14 77-391
Fax +49 7141 14 77-399
kontakt@avedition.de
www.avedition.de

© red dot GmbH & Co. KG
All rights reserved, especially those of translation.
No liability is accepted for the completeness of
the information in the appendix.